WHAT IS GROW?

GROW is a uniquely structured community mental health movement. It began in Sydney, Australia, in April 1957 and has since spread to five other countries - New Zealand, Ireland, the U.S.A. England and Mauritius. It came to Ireland in 1969.

GROW's Programme of Personal Growth, Group Method and Caring and Sharing Community have all been developed from the findings of former mental sufferers in the course of rebuilding their lives after mental breakdown.

Their groups were, in fact, first known as Recovery Groups. This name was subsequently changed to GROW in order to meet the increasing demand for the groups' services in prevention as well as in rehabilitation, and even more broadly for a popular school of life and leadership for mental health.

GROW is anonymous, non-denominational and open to all. Its groups are run by their own members sometimes with the friendly cooperation of a doctor, social worker, minister of religion or any mature member of the community.

GROW groups vary in size from 3 to 15 members.

Meetings are held weekly, last 2 hours, and are followed by refreshments.

No membership fees or dues are charged. No introductions are needed. Just come along.

THE TWELVE STEPS OF PERSONAL GROWTH

1.   We admitted we were inadequate or maladjusted to life.

2.   We firmly resolved to get well and co-operated with the help that we needed.

3.   We surrendered to the healing power of God.

4.   We made personal inventory and accepted ourselves.

5.   We made moral inventory and cleaned out our hearts.

6.   We endured until cured.

7.   We took care and control of our bodies.

8.   We learned to think by reason rather than by feelings and imagination.

9.   We trained our wills to govern our feelings.

10.   We took our responsible and caring place in society.

11.   We grew daily closer to maturity.

12.   We carried the GROW message to others in need.

THE TWELVE STAGES OF DECLINE

1. We gave too much importance to ourselves and our feelings.

2. We grew inattentive to God's presence and providence and God's natural order in our lives.

3. We let competitive motives, in our dealings with others, prevail over our common personal welfare.

4. We expressed or suppressed certain feelings against the better judgement of conscience or sound advice.

5. We began thinking in isolation from others, following feelings and imagination instead of reason.

6. We neglected the care and control of our bodies.

7. We avoided recognising our personal decline and shrank from the task of changing.

8. We systematically disguised in our imaginations the real nature of our unhealthy conduct.

9. We became a prey to obsessions, delusions and hallucinations.

10. We practised irrational habits, under elated feelings of irresponsibility or despairing feelings of inability or compulsion.

11. We rejected advice and refused to co-operate with help.

12. We lost all insight into our condition.

GROW Offices

NATIONAL OFFICE:
11 Liberty St. Cork. Tel. 021 - 277520. Fax. 021 - 273508.

INTERNATIONAL OFFICE:
Cappincur, Tullamore, Co Offaly. Tel./ Fax. 0506 - 41640.

REGIONAL OFFICES:
Dublin: 167 Capel Street, Dublin 1. Tel. 01 - 8734029.
South East: The Ormonde Home, Barrack St. Kilkenny. Tel. 056 - 61624. Fax. 056 - 51615. Also: 4 Canada St. Waterford. Tel. 051 - 57593.
Midlands: The Health Centre, Bury Quay, Tullamore. Tel. 0506 - 51284. Fax. 0506 - 41640. Also: St. Loman's Hospital, Mullingar. Tel. 044 - 40190.
Mid West: 27 Mallow St. Limerick. Tel. 061 - 318813.
Cork/Kerry: 11 Liberty St. Cork. Tel. 021 - 277520. Fax. 02 -1 273508.
West: Tucker St. Castlebar, Co. Mayo. Tel. 094 - 26417.

REGIONAL CONTACTS:
North East: Mary Herr, 48 Cloonevan, Clermont, Dundalk, Co. Louth. Tel. 042 - 21763.
North West: Olive Yashruti, Forquar, Milford, Co. Donegal. Tel. 074 - 53117.

INTERNATIONAL ADDRESSES:
Australia: 209A Edgeware Rd. Marrickville NSW 2204, Australia. Tel. 02 - 5163733. Fax. 02 - 5161503.
U.S.A.: P.O. Box 3667, Champaign, Illinois 61821, U.S.A. Tel. 217 - 352 6989. Fax. 217 - 352 8528530.
United Kingdom: Zena Stokes, 68 Stoke Green, Coventry, West Midlands, England. Tel. 0203 - 455707.

An Introduction by
Minister of State Brian O'Shea

Since its establishment in 1969 GROW Community Mental Health Movement has evolved to become one of the country's largest voluntary mental health movements dedicated to the rehabilitation of former patients of psychiatric hospitals.

The voluntary sector is, of course, an integral and vital element of the health care system of this country and the co-operation which exists between the statutory and voluntary health agencies is of major benefit to the communities which they serve. I am pleased, therefore, to note that GROW has well established lines of communication with health boards and is regarded as a dynamic and committed organisation dedicated to the care of the mentally ill.

This book of personal testimonies will be of enormous benefit not only to those involved in the care of the mentally ill but also to the general public by providing a better understanding of mental illness and highlighting how successful GROW has been in improving the quality of life of its members.

I wish to commend everyone involved in bringing this most worthwhile project to fruition.

Brian O'Shea TD
Minister of State
Department of Health

A foreword
by
Maureen Potter

Since I was invited to become a patron of GROW I must confess I have been a sleeping patron. So I feel a little guilty about writing a foreword to the book. Perhaps this can be my meagre contribution to the remarkable progress of the organisation. GROW certainly has not been sleeping. There are now 90 groups spread all over the country with offices in 8 cities and a national co-ordinator recently appointed.

The growth of GROW is surely an indication of the value of its work in removing the stigma surrounding mental illness. You only have to read the personal testimonies to appreciate how GROW has helped so many people towards recovery. I admire those contributors who have given details of their very personal fears, problems and anxieties in the hope that their stories may help others. Those who set out on the long road to recovery by joining a group and getting the support and encouragement of fellow members were given hope. Please God this book will give hope to many more.

Maureen Potter

Maureen Potter

NOTE:

Wherever the GROW Programme has been quoted the following convention has been followed. Titles of parts of the programme have been given first letter capitals, e.g. The Principle of Personal Value. When other parts have been quoted they have been given single quote marks, e.g. 'I can compel my muscles and limbs to act rightly ...'

Maura's Story

The following is a testimony given by me at the Cork/Kerry region's community weekend in Myross Wood on 11th May, 1996. The theme for the weekend was "Forgiveness".

Just so you all know who I am - my name is Maura. I'm organiser of the Cork City Tuesday night group for my second term. For those who are so interested, I'm still on the right side of thirty and have been a member of GROW for two and a half years.

The story of what led me to GROW goes back, I believe, to my early childhood. I was born into what many people see as a marginalised category, that of disability. I was visually impaired and hard of hearing due to rubella. At a very early age I realised I was different, even from my sister and brother. From the age of about four years I felt I had to prove myself to everyone, including my family. I thought also that I was less lovable than them because I was different.

Because of my eyesight in particular, I was sent away to boarding school to receive a good education. My memories of that time are still vividly and painfully etched on my mind. I recall sitting on a rocking horse crying in the arms of a total stranger. I was eight years old. The feeling of abandonment, complete and utter loneliness, are with me to this day. I blamed my mother for sending me away although, even then, I knew she had no choice. Still, I was very angry with her.

I spent twelve very unhappy years in that school. Apart from loneliness, my initial problem was food. Just to explain - I always had, long before I went to school, a fear of food. I was afraid of putting food into my mouth because it was the wrong colour or a horrible texture. If I took a dislike to food I just could not or would not eat it. Now, this nun was forcing me to eat everything that was set in front of me. If I didn't eat it for dinner I got it for tea and if I didn't eat it for tea I got it for breakfast and so on until I ate it.

While the problem was eventually sorted out by my mother, I still believe that the force feeding aggravated an already present problem, something I will come back to later.

To make matters worse I had much difficulty with my fellow pupils. At the age of fourteen my then "best friend" told me that she and many others thought I was "SLOW". This opened a whole new can of worms. I had always suspected it but being told is quite another story. By then I really did not know or trust my mental ability. My self worth and self confidence were totally destroyed.

Looking back now it's hard to believe I came through it all. I know now that I was quite depressed and anxious during my teens, often thinking of running away, or worse, suicide. Back then I didn't even know the meaning of the word "depression". Instead I felt a complete fool, even more different and alienated than I had before.

I left school at age nineteen to go back home. Whatever dreams I had of having a better life faded fast. My first year home was especially hard. I started a secretarial course but couldn't cope with fellow students. My biggest problem was being totally institutionalised and not knowing the first thing of the "big bad world". As for men, I hardly knew what they looked like, not to mind how to deal with them!!

I got through my course but was unemployed, largely due to an irrational fear of work. After a year and a half I could take no more and moved to Dublin to do a course with Rehab.

My experiences in Dublin were mixed. In some ways Dublin was the beginning of my recovery. It was here I first started to make real friends and lost my fear of getting a job. I went for counselling to try and make some sense of my life and gradually started to learn how to enjoy myself.

The flip side of the coin was food and accommodation. The problem was twofold. Firstly, I was terrified of doing anything that resembled housework in front of my flatmates and, secondly, my fear of food resurfaced. It meant basically that I was not eating properly but I was hiding it. I became terribly secretive and, if questioned, went on the defensive. Many people have asked if I was anorexic. My answer is no, but I do realise I had similar symptoms.

This was the background to my reluctant move to Cork four years ago.

After three years in Dublin I missed it terribly. I carried all my emotional baggage with me and almost immediately ran into trouble with food and accommodation, problems which were inextricably linked to each other. Within two months of moving I was depressed, anxious, not sleeping, not eating and hating myself more by the day for getting myself in the mess I was in.

I couldn't see it then but I realise now that I was in fact very strong. I knew I had to get help so I went back into counselling.

It was two years before I finally heard of GROW. My first impressions were mixed. On one hand the group members were kind and friendly, on the other I thought all this reading and learning from books was utter nonsense. Don't ask me why, but I stayed. Maybe it was the friendship. Maybe I felt I could be someone here. It wasn't until nine months later that it registered that the programme, if applied, could help me. Up to then I had been happily helping choose pieces for everyone else and not working the programme for myself, by myself.

That changed when I was chosen for the Special Activation Project. For the first time I truly saw how the group believed in me and my ability. It also showed me how negative my own feelings towards myself really were. I was still stuck in the attitude that I was really no good and had no ability to improve. I still believed I was "SLOW" and different.

With positive feedback from my group I was able to begin working on my personal value in earnest. I began to see that 'no matter how bad my mental, physical or spiritual condition, I was still a valuable human person'. I also started to normalise my situation by 'being ordinary' and 'doing the ordinary good things'. This, at first, included very simple tasks set by the group including, believe it or not, to boil an egg in someone's company!!

Thereafter, I started looking at my life through Steps 4 and 5 of the GROW programme. 'We took personal inventory and accepted ourselves' and 'We took moral inventory and cleaned out our hearts'. I realised through these that I was one very angry, bitter person. I was angry over being sent away to school, angry over the whole episode of force feeding while in school, angry because my friends had led me to believe I was "slow". Most of all I was angry with myself for allowing people to have such power over me, which meant that I had spent most of my life walking on eggshells because I was afraid of everyone. I knew that the only way to release myself was to forgive these people. It was the key to getting on with the rest of my life, looking to the future, not the past. I had to 'freely forgive from my heart those who had wronged or failed me'.

Doing this was much easier said than done. Just because you say the words "I forgive" does not mean that it happens automatically. Indeed I believe now that forgiveness is a lifelong process that needs continuous work.

I decided to start my journey of forgiveness by looking at those relationships of least importance to me. To forgive my friend I understood that I had to first believe in myself and my ability. I continued, and continue to this day, to work on the principle of Personal Value. I also had to accept that my friend was acting under the influence of her own troubles and was herself misguided.

Next I turned my attention to Sr. X. She too was acting under her own set of circumstances and doing her best at that time. This in itself did not help me. I felt she was to blame for all my later difficulty with food. I needed something more. As a "ritual" I wrote a letter (it was never sent). After writing it I felt completely drained. What came out shocked even me. It was pure poison, undiluted hatred, but it worked. I felt a great release, like as though lead had been removed from around me. Today I feel neither love nor hate. It just is. I cannot change what happened, nor would I wish to. My past is what made me who I now am.

By forgiving that nun I felt less angry with my mother for "putting" me there in the first place. She acted in my best interests, ensuring I got a good education. I could not blame her that facilities were not available to keep me in a school near home. By accepting all this I made my mother my friend. We now have a reasonably good relationship, accepting each other for who and what we are.

When dealing with others, someone said to me that "often what we dislike in others is what we hate in ourselves". This is very true. It is akin to looking in a mirror. This led me to the discovery that, not only had I to forgive others, but I also had to freely forgive from my heart those who wronged or failed me, including MY OWN SELF. The reasons were many. Firstly, I had to forgive myself for living my life the way I had up to then. I also had to forgive myself for allowing people to hold such power over me and, lastly (and most difficult) I had to forgive myself for being disabled. It all came down to accepting myself truly, without reservation for who and what I was.

I soon discovered that, to do this, I had to forgive one more person, God. As I saw it, God was the author of all my ills. If God had created me, why had he made me the way he did? There was a definite element of, why me? I needed to get a 'big idea of God' and to develop a personal relationship with him. It meant developing my spiritual life. I started talking to God. In fact, I started "fighting" with God. Gradually, I found I wasn't as angry. God became a good presence in my life, not just restricted to Catholicism, but an all round picture.

You may well wonder where GROW came into all this. In my group I found a wealth of support and encouragement. I found people who really believed in me and who affirmed this in many ways. By nominating me to be group Organiser they gave me the courage to work on other areas of my life that I once saw as "beyond me".

The Programme which I once saw as "utter nonsense" has proven to be a great help. Some pieces I worked on during my journey are: (a) The Affirmation of Good - to'Truly forgive from our hearts those who have wronged or failed us including our own selves', (b) Prayer for Maturity, (c) Personal Value - believing we are valuable no matter what, (d) Love - 'effective, affective and reflective', (e) Acceptance and Confidence - learning our limitations and utilising our talents, (f) Accepting our Shadow - realising that 'there will always be an undercurrent of fear, anxiety, sadness, etc.', (g) Decentralise - 'seeing the whole picture and not over reacting just because it's happening to me', (h) 'Compelling my muscles and limbs to act rightly in spite of my feelings"'- knowing that just because I feel bad or am afraid that I can still do something, and (i) Feelings - 'feelings are not facts' and 'feelings are like the weather'. I could go on but I think the message is clear.

Since joining GROW my life has changed considerably for the better. On becoming organiser of my group I realised that I was capable of making improvements in other areas of my life. Where once I lived in digs, feeling very frustrated, I now share a house with a friend, doing my own cooking and cleaning and eating normally. As well as holding down a full-time job as a telephonist, I have just completed my first year in U.C.C. under their Adult and Continuing Education Programme. I'm looking forward to receiving my Certificate in Social Studies and doing the Diploma next year. Who knows where I'll go from there? I have a much easier relationship with my family and I've a much more optimistic outlook on life. Recently I've had eye surgery to improve my eyesight a little bit. It has been a huge success, one I am truly delighted with. My disabilities are no longer an issue. I believe GROW was instrumental in helping me to help myself. By its very nature GROW is action. We can talk forever but, if we do not act, we change nothing.

Finally, I am convinced that in choosing the path of forgiveness I released myself from the prison of the past. My bitterness hurt no one but myself. I am no longer stuck in my memories but enjoying the present and looking to the future. Things can only get better. I truly believe that 'the best in life and love and happiness is yet ahead of me'.

Stan's Story

Everyone has a story and it is unique. A complex mosaic studded with people, experiences and events over many years results in a personal history that is far from simple. No amount of detail or analysis can fully exhaust the mystery of any one of us. The following is an attempt to tell a part of my story.

I was born the fifth of ten children in 1931. I had a happy and secure youth. Looking back now I realise I was blessed with good parents. They gave me a great start in life. Hard-working and utterly devoted to their children, I automatically absorbed their faith and practice. Along with that went their politics, prejudices, morals and expectations. When I passed the Leaving Certificate Exam in boarding school at the age of 16, staying at home was not an option. There would be room only for one of us on the farm. And, anyway, farming in the Burren, Co. Clare, held few charms for me. Beautiful scenery and rare flowers weren't the stuff from which one made a living. A few fortuitous or providential encounters resulted in my joining the Redemptorists and when I celebrated my 17th birthday in a strict and structured Novitiate, I was a mere youth, as yet unshaven and prematurely serious. The decision for the priesthood was not a career option. It was a religious call. For me, it was doing God's will. This is what I felt the Almighty wanted me to do with my life and nothing was more important than God in the world of my youth. But that did not make me a new type of human being. Home experiences and home impressions carried into religious life. In fact, they were reinforced there and, to a degree, endure to this day.

Youth is an impressionable time for better or for worse. Probably the single most significant influence in any young life is home, family, parents: the atmosphere, the subtle messages we pick up and the pressures we feel, form and influence us maybe to the day we die. At least, that has been my experience. For example, I'm an achiever. I do a good job. I don't make trouble for authorities or superiors and I mostly get on well with people. The seeds of this life-style were sown in the impressionable years of childhood. I was only seven when I learned that correctness in the presence of authority was vitally important. Unthinking spontaneity could land one in deep trouble. Little attempts at freedom and self-expression backfired or, as I perceived, were frowned upon or belittled.

Once, unexpected, unmerited and, to me, unjust punishment was cruelly meted out in the presence of the whole family. Unaware that my father was within earshot, I said to my younger brother "leave it to hell". "It" was a small article we were arguing about. I had cursed. I had used a swear word. Where did I hear such language? I was court marshalled in the kitchen in the presence of the entire family, humiliated and sent to bed. I was in the dog house and being an outcast, isolated and defeated in a closeknit competitive family was painful. That kind of pain I can feel acutely in similar circumstances today. Contrast that to the day I won three first prizes at the parish sports. As my name was called out, top of the list, I spied my father on the edge of the crowd, pride in his son written large on his face. At home that evening, in the same kitchen, he pronounced me the toast of the family, sat me at the top of the table because I had brought honour to the family name.

Did my young mind conclude that in order to win the approval of significant people, I had to excel, indeed be first! Had I previously concluded that spontaneity, self-expression and independence should be replaced by caution and the clever anticipation of the wishes and expectations of the powerful and strong? At any rate, the acceptance and approval of my father especially, was eagerly sought. It was hard won and, for me, rarely given. Even with the best of parents - and mine were exceptional - we carry baggage into adult life. It's not their fault. They carried their own baggage. What matters is recognising it and dealing appropriately with it.

On the way to the priesthood there were no major crises for the simple reason that I gave no trouble. I was a 'good' student. I kept the rules, did the accepted thing and lived up to expectations of others, especially superiors. It was my natural way of coping. When I was chosen to go to India while still a student, I was not surprised nor, I suspect, was anyone else. I had what I suspect were the usual doubts and worries about celibacy but with the assurance of a confessor/spiritual director, these were disposed of without too much fuss. In June 1957 I was ordained a Redemptorist priest in Bangalore in South India. So, on the threshold of my chosen career, I was strong, healthy, accepted and "successful". A chronic and nagging headache just then rang no alarm bells. It was little more than a nuisance that would not interfere with my life and work.

For about fifteen years I gladly spent the energy and enthusiasm of early manhood in a mountain of activity and involvement. I worked mostly in a southern Indian language, Tamil. The effort at excelling and avoiding mistakes in an alien tongue was huge. All the more, since I was posing as an expert in the rather specialised task of preaching missions and retreats, having only a superficial knowledge of the language. Fatigue and weariness began to claim me as its own. There was always some pain or ache, always some discomforture or unease. A sense of wellbeing, the joy of life, was by now a stranger to me. Appearing in public became more and more a terrifying and unpalatable prospect. But admitting weakness or defeat was unthinkable. Yet the secret fear that I would fail, collapse, be found out, go mad or some worse undefined scenario, lurked not too far beneath the surface.

Of course, I plodded on and muscled through all the commitments and demands on my time and energy. My palms sweated, my mouth went dry, my heart palpitated in panic. I gripped the altar or pulpit so tightly that my knuckles turned white as I held on for dear life. I was a genius at covering up, using ruses like sitting when I dared not even stand for fear of falling. I made sure never to launch out into even telling a story in public lest the need to bail out quickly became urgent. How little I realised then that I was unhealthily self-conscious and giving a prominence and attention to my feelings that was sick and sorry. During these years I was always on my guard lest in a moment of reverie or relaxation I lost control and collapsed. On a few occasions the feeling of sheer terror and utter dejection was more than I could bear or cover up. When I walked off the altar while celebrating Mass or bailed out in the middle of a sermon the sense of failure was extreme. I concluded something must be physically wrong.

A doctor gave me "something to help me". It gave relief and I always give thanks for the gift of medication. I presumed I had been given a tonic to build up an overworked man who was run down. Thousands of pills later, I realised I was being tranquillized almost to the point of addiction. The dependency gripped me to the point where I could not leave the house without my bottle of tranquillizers and if my supply was running low, I panicked, counting the exact number I had left. Now I realised I was suffering from "nerves" and was fully aware of the nature of my pills. But this was my secret. The stigma, the shame and humiliation of being found out as one suffering from "nerves" would be disastrous. So the problem was compounded and the need for cover up and secrecy was all the greater.

Ironically I was more and more "successful" in my ministry. My diary was full and I was in a lot of demand for missions, retreats, talks and seminars. Back in Ireland I was elected and appointed to positions of trust and authority. There were of course periods of remission. The feelings of fear, uneasiness and inadequacy were present with more or less intensity. But I was frequently unutterably tired. Fatigue begot fear and fear became terror during any public appearance. Literally my feet were always physically cold, the spring was going out of my step, the fire was going out of my belly and life was bleak. A blood test around this time revealed a strong and healthy man. Had the diagnosis been leukemia or some measurable or treatable illness, I would have been enormously relieved.

Shakespeare must have experienced some of this when he wrote "how weary, flat, stale and unprofitable seem to me all the uses of this world ... tis an unweeded garden that grows to seed: things rank and gross in nature possess it merely". It amazes me now to think that even when I lost my sleep, after nine years in administration and nearly 25 years in the priesthood, I had no clear insight into my condition. It just never occurred to me that I was physically and emotionally maladjusted and on the verge of nervous collapse. A good night's sleep or a bit of a holiday would soon have put me right as rain, so I thought.

One morning sixteen years ago, on my way to yet another commitment from a crowded calendar, I began to cry. In my adult life I have cried less than half a dozen times. Now the tears began to flow freely and for three days the fear and frustration, the stress and strain, the insecurity and incomprehension of so many years began to drain away. At the end of my tether the barriers came tumbling down. I didn't need to be on my guard anymore. A carefree youth was recalled. Instead of helping, solving, fixing, being involved and responsible for all the churches, I myself needed help and fixing. The innate inadequacy and insufficiency that is our human lot, could now be freely and happily acknowledged. By this time I was in hospital and the next two months - one in hospital and one in convalescence - are today a remote blur. A prolonged break followed before a gradual new confidence replaced the fragile past. I can now give thanks for the breakdown. I don't fear another, but I can give testimony that a breakdown is a breakthrough to a truer and better life.

My story indicates that breakdown is no overnight affair. For me it was many years coming. Neither is there any quick fix or miracle recovery. The seeds were sown in my tender and vulnerable years. My religious training, positive in many respects, did reinforce some unhealthy assumptions and prejudices. Recovery then is a long haul and I'm still pulling and will happily do till my dying day. Hospital and medication helped initially to unwind, relax and recover the gift of sleep. How we take the simple and beautiful things for granted! Beginning to sleep naturally again was like being born again. Also, I give thanks for a wise doctor whose aim with medication was to end its use as soon as possible. Mercifully, within months, that particular support had done its work. More enduring supports were my community, my family and my close friends. These latter provide nourishment that is sustaining because it is permanently on tap. But, for me, the greatest single help towards personal understanding and growing back to mental health was GROW.

What Alcoholics Anonymous is for the alcoholic, GROW is for the sufferer from "nerves". Like A.A. it is anonymous, non-denominational and open to all. It has 12 Steps of Personal Growth and indeed 12 Stages of Decline. These Steps and all GROW wisdom are the recorded helps and hindrances of Growers over the past 40 years. Out of this has evolved the GROW Programme and the GROW Group Method. GROW is simply a no-nonsense, common sense programme for living that prevents breakdown as well as pointing the way to mental health. The similarity with A.A. is not surprising since the first GROW members were originally members of A.A.

I can still recall the hesitations, the weighing of pros and cons before attending my first GROW meeting. What would it be like? An acquaintance who now runs a successful alcoholic treatment unit, first told me about GROW and assured me I would feel at home there. But what would they think? A priest suffering from nerves! And in my mind I was no ordinary priest! I was posted in Limerick at the time and when I eventually took my courage in my hand and went to the Social Service Centre in Henry Street, I was enormously relieved when the receptionist told me the meeting that night was cancelled. Another month passed before I had the courage to try again. I have been a more or less regular member ever since.

In GROW I have come to cherish some of the most remarkable people I have met in my life. They are people with the truest kind of courage. Nearly always afraid or anxious or depressed they struggle to do the most ordinary things - getting up in the morning, meeting people in the street, buying a single item in a shop. Add to that the extraordinary tasks of rearing a family, earning a living, relating to family, colleagues, friends. Yet they heroically and doggedly do what they must to lead ordinary and fruitful lives. Some suffer relapse, some have the disappointment of needing to return to hospital yet again. But they begin again and slowly but surely grow into healthy people who manage and take control of their lives. They are husbands and wives, workers and unemployed, college students and professionals. We have the down and outs and the up and outs. The GROW Programme, the meeting, the method, and friendship of the group have been and are a support beyond my expectations. I now count among my friends people who have been hospitalised, received shock treatment, been heavily drugged and lived in depression for many years. So many of them have left all that behind and know that the best in life and love and happiness is yet to come.

For myself, I list what I found particularly helpful in GROW.

1. The friendly and caring atmosphere that respects and takes seriously each person. GROW's essential faith is in the person and his/her radical goodness. Social status, profession, political or religious affiliation don't matter. A member shares at his/her own pace and time. What is said is strictly confidential to the group.

2. The wisdom of the programme, the trust generated in the group and the highly structured form of the meeting is impressive. A social cuppa after the meeting is the time for chat and other news but the meeting itself excludes irrelevant talk. I always feel the meeting is constructive and time well spent.

3. At a personal level I had many learnings. It was not easy to admit, even to myself, that for years I had given far too much importance to my feelings, that I was unhealthily competitive, that another's success did not diminish me, that I was an ordinary human being, but I did have 'a unique and personal value.'. Any special gift would flower if solidly based on the truth that I share a common humanity with all my brothers and sisters in the human family.

4. The causes of breakdown are complex and manifold. But blaming the past, a popular media ploy, is a barren exercise. Parents, teachers, priests, employers, authority figures etc., surely left some mark or scar on me. Life is like that. Forever making them responsible for my present hang-ups, is a cop out from taking responsibility for my life now. Whoever, whatever, whenever - caused me to be fearful, anxious, panic prone, depressed etc., it is my task, duty, responsibility to be up and doing and using the helps to get better.

5. Maybe the greatest learning was the need for patience. The sixth step reads We endured until cured. It takes time to reach breakdown stage. Healing and cure is about change - deep change involving thinking, talking, relationships, behaviour. The Gospel term is "conversion". Who likes change or finds it easy! It is something like trying to shed a language one has thought in and spoken for years and now deliberately opting for a new tongue. Dramatic, overnight change is suspect, without roots. Healthy enduring change is so gradual as to be almost inperceptible. It is measured in months rather than weeks, even years rather than months.

6. Like so many in GROW I have a sensitive and perfectionist nature. Like every other human being I never achieve perfection and feel the consequent failure acutely. GROW has a simple wisdom that is as deceptive as it is challenging. For this particular ailment it says 'If a thing is worth doing it is worth doing badly - for a start, and while you're improving'. Could anything be sounder or simpler!

7. At the end of the day health is a gift. It is received not achieved. While engaging in the programme, doing practical tasks, attending the meetings etc., I had to relax and not force what cannot be forced. Sleep for example. I needed to prepare for sleep, eliminate distractions, be generally comfortable and so on, but then I had to allow sleep to steal up on me. None of us goes to sleep, sleep comes to us. A hard lesson to learn for a strong achiever! The same goes for general health.

8. GROW is unashamedly politically incorrect when it affirms that prayer and God/Higher Power/Supreme Being/He/She/It is essential to recovery. Reflection, meditation and prayer have assumed a renewed importance in my life. Attending to the spiritual/mystical dimension is vital. A significant part of breakdown is a deep hunger and thirst which, if not satisfied, leads to emptiness, boredom, frustration and depression. So easy to neglect the spiritual for seemingly "good" reasons - overactivity, over preoccupation with self, over anxiety, over-conscientiousness etc. In Grow we attend to the physical, intellectual and emotional, the spiritual is assuredly not neglected.

GROW is a programme for living. It simply is classified common sense. Breakdown is just a dramatic reminder of what is basic and necessary for everyone, namely GROWs trinity - Truth, Friendship, Character. I warmly recommend it.

Doris's Story

My name is Doris and I am twenty-four years old. As far as I can remember I was always a nervous person. It was while going to school that all my problems began. My mother drank a lot so there was a lot of tension in my family. I had no brothers or sisters so I grew up very much alone until I started school. I worried a lot as a child and could be described as a nervous individual.

There was always a lot of tension between myself and my mother. At such an early age I couldn't really understand why she drank, or why she behaved the way she did. It seemed very much to me at the time to be all on purpose. I couldn't see any other reason for it.

I got on fairly well at school, but never really found myself being happy there. I was always picked on a lot by the other students, because I was always too quiet and never stood up for myself. I was referred to as ugly and fat and I developed a terrible shame and embarrassment about my physical appearance. This made me feel ugly and I began to believe I was ugly and physically unattractive. I can remember those years as being very painful and they left me with a lot of bad memories.

When I went into secondary school I got on very well studywise. The girls in the class were all very nice and I really liked it there. After a while the teachers began to notice how good I was and decided to promote me into a higher grade, as I was in a Group Cert. class. I was encouraged to go, so I did. It was definitely a mistake and something I regretted very much. The girls were not as friendly, and did not really like me for getting on. They expressed their dislike of me by passing comments and making sure that I heard them, mostly just making fun of me. I was quiet and just preferred to get on with my work instead of causing trouble, I was always so full of fear, so afraid of rocking the boat.

25

I got as far as Inter Cert and I had been getting sick every morning at the thoughts of going into school. I didn't take any notice of this and thought it would just go away if I ignored it for long enough. I was also very anxious about things and I became scrupulous about small things, such as putting out lights, putting my books in my bag. I would go back to check each time, to see if I had done everything 'perfectly'. It was a ritual of self-torture, checking and re-checking, each time feeling that if something was out of place disaster would strike, that somehow if I could arrange everything perfectly, have everything perfectly in place I might begin to feel better about myself and stop this mental torture!

I went back to fifth year and had intended doing my Leaving Cert. However, the first week back I began to get sick again, this time not just getting up every morning, but even at school. I couldn't even keep my breakfast down at this stage. Things were so different. I found the work very hard and as classes had been changed so were the people and teachers, and I was moved away from most of my friends.

After about a week I decided I'd leave. I thought this would solve my problem, but it didn't. All my teachers were against me for my decision. Nobody at this stage knew what the real problem was. Nobody it seemed was on my side and it would take forever to describe how I felt at that time, all I knew was that I had been told I made a very bad mistake and that I had, to quote my Vice Principal at the time, "thrown away a golden opportunity". It was like a living nightmare. If I didn't do my Leaving Cert. it was the end of the world, so it seemed at that time. No matter how hard I tried I could not summon up the courage to face going back to school. I was paralysed by fear.

A few weeks later my doctor came to see me as I had stopped going out anywhere. He told me what my problem was, there and then - it really shocked me. I was suffering from anxiety (agoraphobia), that was why I was getting sick all the time while going out. He suggested I see a psychiatrist and I refused, thinking that if I did that I would be admitting I was MAD. He did not force me, respecting that it was my decision and asked me if I wished to take something to help me. I jumped at the idea and realised only much later that I made a big mistake.

For the next year and a half or so I tried to get by pretty much on my own. I joined a prayer group and found this a great help at this particular time. However, as time went on I knew I could not do it all on my own, and having eventually overcome my terrible fear of psychiatrists I went to my G.P. and requested to be referred to one. At first I found them no help whatsoever. I was then sent to a psychologist as well as attending the psychiatrist. Both of these had very different ideas as to what would help me, so I was in a situation where I was, in my description, 'the meat between the sandwich', for some time.

When the psychiatrist tried taking me off the medication my own G.P. prescribed I found out how bad I really was. I realised only then the tablets were masking the extent of the problem. I was fooling myself into thinking that what I was suffering with was very slight. The panic attacks became unbearable and it got to the stage where I felt that there was no hope for me. It was then, when I was finding none of these people (psychiatrist, psychologist) a help, that I decided to go privately to another psychiatrist whom I heard was very good. He gave me the medication that helped me to stop getting sick. I then, under his supervision began to move out a bit and fight the panic attacks. After a month or so I was much improved.

A couple of months later I went on work experience which unfortunately didn't work out. It was then that I joined GROW. I found everybody there to be very friendly and I really felt I had support. I learnt from the Blue Book how to be more positive, not to allow my feelings to stop me from doing something just because I was afraid. I began to stop living by my feelings and imagination. I learnt to let go and eventually my self-confidence improved. I was no longer in bondage to the awful anxiety that had ruled and dominated my life for so many years. All of this however did not come overnight, but gradually my life was becoming normal. I had my setbacks now and then but I was always encouraged to get up and try again. I joined a youth prayer group, where I met some wonderful friends of my own age who went through the very same as I did at school, so I wasn't so different after all.

I owe a lot of my recovery to GROW. I owe it also to my family and friends who supported me through some very trying times. My relationship with my mother has never been better, she gave up drinking years ago, and we're like sisters now. I started a secretarial course and this seemed to suit me. I know one very important thing: 'If there's hope for me, there's hope for anyone'.

I was able to face some exams in typing, word processing and book-keeping and I got great results. I was very nervous at first. I thought I could never face exams in the future and I had a terrible sense of failure and fear of failure in my life. Through GROW I learnt that it's not the results that mattered it was the fact that I faced the thing that I feared unreasonably and even if I had failed it wouldn't have mattered. The lesson I was learning in GROW was that I shouldn't be afraid to fail because it's a necessary part of life. The person who fails and who brushes himself/herself off and starts again is a person of great character even if he/she never succeeded in anything they could at least say "I'm an expert TRIER". The fact that I did face what I feared despite my feelings of impending doom and anxiety is what I am most proud of in the end. The Three Basic Determinations were an invaluable source of help during this time.

Since finishing the secretarial course I have succeeded in holding down various jobs which were offered to me. My confidence in my working capabilities has improved enormously. I have to thank all those employers who, knowing of my background still chose to put their trust in me, and thank God it has not been in vain. At present I am working part time as a secretary at the Camphill Community and this Christmas, 1996 will be my second year with them.

I am firmly convinced that God brought me to GROW and that GROW was the answer to my prayers for help. I can see, looking back, how he used both the programme, but most especially the people in the group as instruments to mould and shape me into the person I have become.

I have had my good times and my bad times over the last few years. I still, from day to day, have to struggle with the problems and frustrations of life, but being in the GROW group, being able to share these ups and downs, gives me great strength to keep climbing. Its ordinary to struggle -its growthful - its life. I suppose I now view my life as a journey, but I travel with friends, people who also have challenges, setbacks, disappointments but who still feel life is worth living. If I had isolated myself over the last few years I most certainly would have slipped down the slippery slope into depression. Being in GROW has certainly prevented me, many times, from giving up, on my road back to recovery.

I am encouraged when someone in the group comes along and begins to improve in their lives and their outlook on life. Especially those who have had very serious labels like that of "manic depressive" or "schizophrenic" and to see, despite the odds and the prophets of doom, their obvious well being and growing to maturity. It gives me hope and a reason to rejoice both for them and for the inspiration they give.

At present I am learning to drive, which will help me to become more independent. The step I am working on is Step 11 - We grew daily closer to maturity. Many people ask me if I ever hope to leave GROW. For the foreseeable future the answer is no. I see GROW as an important part of my life, a growing community of people. I value the people and the friendships I have made both in the groups and outside of the groups. We're just ordinary people, a club of people, who have a lot in common when it comes to our daily struggles with our feelings and our tendencies to slip now and then down the slope of decline. We all manage somehow to keep our little boats afloat. I suppose I could sum up by quoting a 'one liner' I read on the first poster I ever saw advertising GROW. It had a picture of a small group of people sitting in a circle and underneath was written 'You alone can do it, but you can't do it alone'.

I will finish my story with a similar line to the above one but with my own personal interpretation of it, 'I alone did it, but I didn't do it alone!'

Jack's Story

I had never been to any group meetings of any kind when I first came to GROW through an adult education exhibition, and I was totally unaware of any "programme" or "meeting method". I thought GROW was solely a platform for people to discuss their problems. To be honest, I never thought about the "challenge" that GROW or "problems" could raise. The "challenge to action", in my opinion, is the greatest gift that GROW members can give to each other.

In 1992 I joined GROW, and I have not looked back. My problems are not all solved, quite the contrary, but I have the knowledge of realising that so many people suffer, and in that way, having problems makes me think we are the lucky ones, being able to confide in each other and trust each other, while there are many other people out there who are carrying so much "mental baggage" on their own, without friends or family. In 1992 I felt I had come to the end of my life. I had tried so many things to get better, I didn't know what was wrong with me, and I was so alone. I had many friends and family, but I was alone in the sense that I had obsessive fears and knew no-one who had experienced this type of "illness". I would worry compulsively about things and everyone would say "just forget about it". At that point I was alone.

I had a good job, a beautiful girlfriend, sufficient money and a new car. I had finally arrived at a point in my life that I had always wanted. I was happy. But one night I got a severe panic attack and could not come out of it. I kept thinking I might have knocked someone down with my car. In reality, I knew I hadn't, but my mind began to trick me. For a few years my life would be a story of one panic attack like this after another. Everything became so serious - the joy was gone from my life.

Now, looking back on my early years, I know I had many panic attacks in my childhood, but I didn't know there was a "term" to describe these feelings. I am the youngest of four children, and my father was a "martyr for the drink". He wasn't violent, but he was the boss and we were very much afraid of him. But we loved him too. My mother was a most innocent lady, like someone born 50 years before her time. She helped everyone she could, always doing charity work, feeding old people etc., but after my father died, she too drank for a few years. This is hard in normal circumstances, but we also had the added burden of running a bar. My mother always denied she drank, and so there was a lot of shame, guilt and fear associated with her drinking. When I was 10 I had a birthday party, but all I remember is my brother grabbing a brandy bottle from my mom and I was so embarrassed. I had adopted my mother's belief that sickness was to be hidden, denied and absolutely not to be told to the neighbours or friends. I told no one my mom drank, I was faithful to her secret, but everyone knew anyway.

I was the dreamer in my family. I would hide myself away for hours on end reading a book or playing or sleeping in cupboards or the hot press. I was small and could curl myself up like a cat and no-one would find me in my dream world. Reality was too hard to bear, there were too many problems, so I, like all other children, made my own world of happiness. There were always things in my life I wanted to change - and they were big things at the time. I was so fat at one stage I really hated it. I was small and wanted to be taller. I wanted a house in the country, not the city. I wanted to be really good-looking.

Over the years my mom got much better, but drink was still a taboo subject, so it was never mentioned. I think I had many fears bottled up because of the denials. All our problems, in fact we were told, would be alright in time and with God's help, but nothing ever practical was done about them.

I studied very hard for my leaving certificate, but when the exam came I was too hyper and didn't get the results I could have got. During one exam I got very panicky and so after that I felt I had failed. I wanted to die, my life was hell. But after the leaving cert I forgot about these panic attacks and this was typical of me. I would get very upset about things for a few days and then forget about the problem and move on to the next attack.

But in 1991 I got myself into a panic attack I couldn't get out of. I had everything but couldn't stop thinking that everything I did could affect people. If I cut the grass someone might trip over a blade of grass and hurt themselves. My world became hell. Other people would laugh at things they were doing if it wasn't right, whereas I would start to worry about it. I began washing my hands compulsively, checking and rechecking switches in case of fire, and driving back to places I had just come from to check if the pothole was really a pothole or someone I had knocked down. There were hundreds of obsessions but all had the common denominator that I could, or might, hurt someone, and I couldn't live with that.

I tried psychotherapy, which cost me an arm and a leg - no good. I tried psychologists - not as expensive but also not very good for ME. I tried suicide on a few occasions, but I couldn't do it. I kept asking myself "what's wrong"?

So I came to GROW and I listened attentively. I had found an oasis in a desert. I received the reading on Maturity, which talks about 'the vigour and peace of a person who is wholly attuned to reality', which was very inspiring. I learned the Blue book off by heart practically.

For me the 5 Keys for Understanding Feelings became very important. I realised that all my thinking was based on imagined feelings and 'feelings are not facts'. This in itself was very consoling. I was always looking for a reason why I shouldn't exist, but Bedrock put paid to that - 'Whatever the trouble, (imagined or real), it is one of those things that can and do happen to human beings, and God, who made me, can help me overcome every evil that affects my life'.

Of course, like so many people, my greatest problem was LACK OF SELF ESTEEM, so I daily say the Personal Value lines - 'no matter how bad my physical, mental or spiritual condition, I am still a human person' and 'my life has meaning'. Also a very important principle of GROW to me is Reasonableness. I am a type of perfectionist and so, if I am " reasonable", then I have to accept imperfection. This is great for perfectionists. We 'aid and require others to be reasonable' , thus we can make mistakes - but it's O.K. - mistakes are an exercise of love.

Of course the creme de la creme of GROW for me are the 4 Stabilizing Questions. I used to spend evenings worrying about things that I thought I should worry about. But the 4 stabilizing questions put a specific tag on my thinking. I have to 'be definite - what exactly am I troubled about?'

and 'be rational'. If my problem is not certain I have to leave it and, in so far as I can, think about something else.

I am someone who thought I could never have happy times again. I still have tough times, but the good days really pay off for the bad ones. My life has meaning which is wonderful. Sometimes I am so happy it hurts.

After I was in GROW for some time I "challenged myself to action" and realised that 'telling the untellable"to someone is really helpful. I talked and talked to my friends, and through an alternative therapist, I realised my problem was that I had some bisexual tendencies, which I was so afraid of. I had no place for this in my life and so I couldn't bring myself to think of it. I loved my girlfriend with all my heart, so my mind couldn't bring itself around to thinking about this problem. I was in a no win situation and so my mind thought of everything it could in order to prevent me from realising this secret.

These days I'm not great about talking about this, but I am learning. I've got a problem and that's good'. I am doing the very best I can and asking God daily to 'teach me to see things as they really are', and 'to accept myself'.

When we accept ourselves, no one except ourselves can ever rob us of our mental health again.

Kitty's Story

My name is Kitty. I am 62 years old and I must say that the last four years are the best I've had since I married forty years ago. My reason for saying this is that I had been suffering from depression for over thirty years. Frank and I married in England. I was a happy person then. We returned soon after to my home place in North Clare and it is then that my problem began. We started our family of seven children and as time went by I was getting less and less happy with myself and with people around me. I went to my doctor and she put me on Valium and I was on them for twenty years. Each time I went to the doctor she increased the dosage until I was on the strongest dose permitted. Life was just misery. I would go to bed (I won't say at night because I never stayed there at night). I'd pray that I would never wake up again. I spent most of my days in bed feeling sorry for myself and just to be alone. I could not stand to be around the house when Frank and the family were talking or laughing, because I thought it was about me.

Ten years ago I changed my doctor and he wanted me to go into the local psychiatric hospital. To me that was the worst thing he could have said. I thought you needed to be mad to be sent to these places and what about the stigma? Eventually I was put into hospital and went through many different treatments and medication in an attempt to solve my problem. The next six years were not much better. I always felt a big lump in my chest and it seemed to be getting worse. I often took the carving knife and put it to my chest to make an opening and get whatever was there out, but I hadn't the courage to dig deep.

One night four years ago I saw a programme on TV, it mentioned support groups and what I heard about GROW in particular appealed to me. I felt it would be good if I could go to something like that. Then I found

GROW. The first meetings meant nothing to me, I found them hard to follow and I often went home feeling worse. After about six months I really settled down and began working the programme. The first task I was asked to do was to ignore the big lump in my chest. GROW taught me who I was and where I was going. I got back my personal value and a sense of what I was worth. I began to see things as they should be seen and I also learned that I was not the only one with problems. A lot of people felt as bad as I did and I could talk to them openly. I have made some wonderful friends in GROW. There is one person in the group, Tom our organiser, that I have to thank in particular for the wonderful support and help and the constant contact between meetings which is very important.

As I was improving gradually and on the way up, my mother died in 1991 and I was really shattered. The psychiatrist wanted to increase my medication, but the group was wonderful and I was encouraged to have the courage to grieve. The group set a task for me to talk to my doctor about this and I didn't take any additional medication. The group helped me to help myself more than any pills would. As time passed I saw the programme in action and the progress other people were making. Some were phasing out medication and some came off it completely.

In February 1992 I talked to the group about coming off medication. I was encouraged to have a go and also to seek the support of my doctor. She agreed because, as she said, she could see the strides I had made since I joined the group. I had changed from being the helpless patient to being able to decide what I wanted. I achieved my goal gradually and moved completely off medication by 16 November 1992. First it was one day at a time and then the days grew into weeks. I had to work even harder at the programme then, because of little setbacks now and then.

The real test of the quality of my recovery came in July 1993 when I had a very bad break in my ankle. I spent a month in an orthopaedic hospital. It was then I really found out how the programme had helped me. My spiritual growth helped me to surrender myself to God during the long and painful months that followed. My friends in the group were always there for me, the phone calls and the visits kept me going. I thank God that I had the years in GROW before all this happened, otherwise I would not have come through it so well.

I am now four years in GROW. I am a well person again, doing the things I missed out on for thirty years. I am off all medication since No-vember 1992. So now at night when I say my prayers, I thank God and GROW for how well I am, I want to live to be a hundred. I also want to thank Frank for all his help and patience. To anyone in GROW who says it will not come together for them, I say to them work at the programme. No one can do it for us - we have to do it ourselves but the help is there and it's a wonderful feeling to be well and able to enjoy life again. I can-not thank enough everyone in GROW who helped me. I am there now to give that help back.

Frank's Story

My name is Frank. I was born in Ennistymon 63 years ago. I grew up a very happy child right into manhood. Like all good fellows I got to know a lovely girl, later to become my wife. We went to London and married there in 1954. Her father asked me to return to look after his farm as he was in bad health. We returned to Doolin in March 1955. I started to work on the land and soon things began to improve for me as I loved the country and it's way of life. Kitty did not like returning but I told her it would work for us. My life was fulfilled.

Our first child was born in June 1956, a girl. In November 1957 our son was born. October 1957 Kitty's father died and that was a big shock for both of us. It closed the door on us ever going back to London. Things started to go wrong for Kitty soon after that. She became unhappy with her life and began to blame me for returning home. I did not give her much heed as I could not understand how a person could be unhappy in such a beautiful place. I worked harder to try and make it up to her but it did not fill the longing in her heart for London. The children came quickly until we had our family of seven.

I got a big break. I was given a job for three years with time off to do the farm work. I then thought all my problems were over. Constant money every week and again a better way of life. Still the rows continued and her mother always stood up for me. She could see I was doing my best to make a better living for all of us. She often said that if I was coming home drunk or breaking all in the house or kicking her around she would have something to grumble about. I have to say even though Kitty and myself had plenty of rows, she was always kind to her mother. All she would say is "Take his part. To you he is perfect."

The family grew up and I grew with them and we had great times together. Kitty grew away from them. She thought we were always talking and laughing at her. She saw her GP constantly and she was on valium for many years at this stage. I often told her the tablets were making her worse but her reply was that I did not know what I was talking about. The family started to go away to make a life for themselves and things got worse. I often thought to pack the whole lot in and go back to England myself. I married her for better or worse, in sickness and in health. I could not fathom out how such a lovely person as Kitty was when we got married could be so cruel to me. I could not do anything right in her eyes. I got sick myself and had to go to my own doctor. I had a cough and pains in my chest and felt very low in myself. I asked the doctor if I was going mad as I could not make sense any more of what was happening. I told him about the rows with Kitty and all that was happening between us. I told him I could go no further and asked his help. He was sorry for me and said he would cure my cough and pains. He told me he would help Kitty but I had to get her to agree to see him. I told her the doctor wanted to see her to get the flu injection. My next visit she came with me. The doctor spoke to Kitty and asked her to see a psychiatrist. We duly went and she put her on medication. They worked for a while. Again back to the psychiatrist, this time to be put in hospital. I was blamed for this also. In Kitty's mind I was now free to do as I wanted. My wife was mad so she did not have rights any more. At this stage I lost all confidence in myself, in God, and in all things around me. I cried many times on my own looking for some sign to let me know things were all right. It came in many ways. Frankie and Ann (my son and daugther) knew what I was going through and I could talk to them. Mrs. Lynch prayed for me and again I found my God in many places and in the people around me. I held my head high and marched on as best I could. I was very involved in parish work such as Pioneers and Old Folks parties and outings, choir and all things to do with the church. When people told her how good I was to them she never praised me only found fault, saying I could help everyone but her. At this stage we were fighting every day, long periods of silence from two to five days, no dinner when I came from work. I was blamed for everything that upset her. I could not talk to her as she would not listen to me. At this stage I thought if she had a holiday it might help. Frankie and Ann were involved at this stage and having a very hard time. Even though they were very good to their mother they could not understand how she changed. I had £500 to give Kitty for a holiday. Before the ticket was booked I got a chance to ask her if she would like a break with her sisters in London. I told her what we intended to do and I was sorry as my world fell apart. She hit the roof. We were "putting her mother in a home for old people and selling the house and land, dividing the money between us and leaving her with nothing!" The next three months were pure hell, like living with the devil. We could not talk, laugh or be seen together as we "were trying to get rid of her.".

Slowly I gained her confidence back and things settled down a bit. Then she saw Check-Up on television. I did not see the programme myself as I was doing other work. A row when I came in. I was told about the programme and "being me, KnowAll, did I know about it?" I had never heard about GROW. I got her to calm down a bit and said I would enquire all about it. I asked her if she intended to go to the meetings. We attended our first meeting in Ennis in April 1990. I thought the meetings were very good. I could understand everything that was going on. I got the blue book and started reading it. I knew it all as I had done all it said. As I studied the programme I knew I had a lot to learn, to act rightly in spite of how I felt. The Three Basic Changes are my favourite as I believe they have changed my whole life. Why am I in Grow?, Have a big idea of God. Many more are also big on my list. Time moved on. Here I have to praise the people that had the courage to accept me in GROW I am grateful to you. Kitty attended three meetings but did not get much from them. I went to the fourth meeting on my own, she would not come. Next day I was asked all about who was in, how many we had. I told her if she wanted to know about GROW the car was going every Monday night and to be in it.

Kitty was talking one night about me and I did not like what I was hearing. I answered of course and across the table I was told to shut up and let her talk. I did not like that at all. My first lesson in learning the programme. Later I was to learn that everybody gets a chance to speak and in that way restore confidence, also the problems could be debated and solved. I could see a change in Kitty for the first time in many years. She was reading her book and listening to her tape, also doing her tasks and agreeing with me a bit more. For myself, I was learning to accept that I had taken her world away from her when I had said we would never go back, only told her if she wanted to go to take herself away.

After six months of struggling we had come a long way. My reward came suddenly when Kitty said one night she was wrong and that neither I nor the children were laughing or talking about her. That night I felt a great weight lifted from my whole being. Also I realised that I had a bigger task placed on me to build that person back to mental health. That has been my aim in GROW for 3 and a half years. I am very proud of her and what she has done. I am very proud to belong to GROW and be able to help my fellow Growers back to full health again. I am here to give back the help I got myself, hope, friendship and love. I am a victim of depression and I keep in touch with the group. They will not let you down in good times or in bad.

Kitty broke her ankle 15 months ago. She has endured long days on her own. Here again the group were like our family with visits, phone calls and help in every way possible. I have changed my life and the things that I thought important are only my dreams. I have found a whole new set of values and a new person also. We are growing back together again, working for one another instead of going our own ways. There is no bitterness, no jealousy, no blame between us. I have found the girl I lost 35 years ago and she is going nowhere without me. I am a very lucky man indeed. Without GROW this would never be possible, so I say "you alone can do it, but you can't do it alone".

Since I wrote this story I have taken on the task of Recorder in one of the Ennis groups. Normally I don't attend many meetings during summer months as I have a farm to attend to. But now I am committed to my position in GROW and I attend all year round. I have a greater understanding of the programme and it gives me great satisfaction to hear fellow Growers giving the same advice that I myself gave them. I am humble enough to realize that I need help myself, from time to time. Kitty lost her mother and also broke her ankle. I also have been very sick and lost my mother. All this has deeply affected our lives but with the help of friends in GROW, we have grown stronger and closer together.

I have made some wonderful friends in GROW, especially our fieldworker Breda, a loving and caring person. She has been down the road of despair and sorrow but has put it all behind her, with the help of GROW. I must say "thanks" to Brigid and Paula for their help and encouragement when I was very low- friends like these are very rare. GROW has given me all that I am today, it has given me back my wife, my home and above all my peace of mind. Kitty and I were lost without GROW. It has done for Kitty what 35 years of medication and doctors failed to do.

Christine's Story

My name is Christine and I have been a member of GROW for over nine years. When I first joined I was taking sixteen tablets a day and suffering from severe depression and anxiety.

My problems started at a very young age because of a squint I had in my eyes. I was constantly called names by my school friends. I was tenth in a family of twelve children so I came in for a bit of name calling at home as well. I reckon because of this my confidence was never given a chance from the word "go". Even at that very young age I was starting to isolate myself and hated when I was put out to play with other children. My thoughts were never that of a child, they were constantly taken up with "How will my mam pay the bills?", "Will my dad always have a job?" and "Will the trouble in the North come down here"? Consequently, I suffered from depression at about the age of nine. I didn't know what it was but it hurt me inside and I could not explain why. I went into my teenage years with such low self esteem that I became a 'Yes' person. I never believed anyone could like me for being me, so I thought that if I bought the biggest presents and did the most favours and of course, kept saying 'yes', that they would. I constantly compared myself to others and they always came out on top. I never felt that I was of any worth.

I met my husband at a very young age and I married when I was seventeen. Shortly after I had my first baby. For the first time in my life I experienced peace - here was someone I felt so much love for and I didn't have to say a word. The peace didn't last very long because shortly after Donna's birth I started to suffer the dreaded panic attacks. I was so frightened at first because I thought I was dying and I was running to the doctor every second day. I was put on tranquillizers from the word "go". From there on and for the next seven years my life became a vicious circle of phobias and obsessions. I can see now how one just triggered off the next. I became obsessed with my health - it was never just a pain in my chest or a headache - it was always a heart attack or a tumour. It got so bad that if I heard of an illness on Monday I would have all the symptoms by Friday and, of course, be dying by Sunday. Because of this I developed a fear of the night, so I would stay awake all night and would only feel safe when the day came. To kill the time at night, in which I will never forget the loneliness, I started to clean the house and this was to become my greatest madness. I would clean the house from top to bottom and when I'd finish I would start all over again. Jobs that ordinary people only did a couple of times a year, I was doing every day. I couldn't sit still for a moment and I would search for things to do. My husband would come home in the evening for his dinner and I would stand in front of him until he'd finished. I would go so far as to be lifting his plate and wiping under it if he dropped something. If I gave a visitor a cup of tea I would be in a state of panic until they would finish, the need to wash the cup was so great. By now I had my second child and between the children and my husband I reckon their lives were pretty miserable. I was forever giving out about the house and demanding that they keep the place tidy. I hated things like their birthday parties. The thoughts of lots of people in my house would petrify me. My husband tried to help but under the circumstances there wasn't a lot he could do. Again I had completely isolated myself. I never confided in any of my family, not even my mam whom I loved.

Because of my obsession with cleanliness I developed anorexic tendencies. I would go all day without eating just in case I dirtied the worktop or a plate. I would only cook when I had to and it got so bad that I went all day forgetting to eat. After being this way for a while the food wouldn't pass my throat. Suicide had crossed my mind several times by now, both my physical and mental health had gone to pieces. I weighed less than seven stone. I couldn't sleep or eat and I was taking tranquillizers non stop. I would have been happy to die, I felt I had suffered enough.

It was on coming home from a stay in hospital that I heard about GROW. My mam had heard about it on the radio and she suggested that I go along. She was very upset, as were all my family, they never realised I was so sick. How could they? I had become a great actress. My memories of that first night are of three people from Cork in a room of about 40/50 people, trying to have a meeting. Ann was giving her story and for the first time I heard the words 'you can and will become completely well" from The Principle of Hope, which is so important to anyone starting out. I couldn't believe what she was saying because I had been told that I would be on medication for the rest of my life because of a chemical imbalance. It was these words that brought me back for the next few meetings. It was so hard for me at the beginning because I had completely lost my concentration and my ability to hold a conversation or make eye contact, so I kept my head down and my mouth shut. I was there for about six months before I spoke and that started with me crying my eyes out. Because of my ongoing suicidal thoughts and my weight loss I was to go back to hospital on a particular Friday. I sat at that meeting and all I could think about was going to the river - I felt that I had been taken over by some force that was going to drag me there. I felt as if it wasn't me anymore in my body. This was one of my strangest experiences. I don't know where I got the courage from that night but I told the group of my thoughts and that night I was given my first task which was to eat one nourishing meal a day no matter how long it took me to get it down - to keep saying over and over again 'Never say I can't if it's an ordinary and a good thing' from the Three Practical Points of Control. I will never forget how hard that group fought to keep me out of hospital. Every couple of hours there was someone on the phone offering words of comfort and support. From then on I took my tasks very seriously. The Three Basic Determinations became my prayer, especially the words 'I will go by what I know, not by how I feel" which I still use every day. Gradually my appetite started to improve which saved me from going back to hospital. Patience was a very big problem at the time, so for about twelve months my ongoing task was Step 6 - We endured until cured. I had to accept that I had a lot of problems and that it would take time to sort them out. The words 'my feelings will get better as my habits of thinking and acting get better' were said a hundred times a day. I will forever be grateful to that group for all the help they gave me, especially Pat and Ned, who took no nonsense and handed out tasks every week. They taught me that 'there is no natural way to instant good feelings' and it's the small steps and 'the repetition of many acts' that will get you there.

I have been brought to my knees several times before GROW, by an overwhelming conviction that I had nowhere else to go. GROW has given me back my life and it has enabled me to stand on my own two feet and deal with most things I come up against. It is seven years since I've taken any tablets and I've never had the confidence that I have now. The most wonderful gift it has given me is how to relate to other people, especially my father, a person I had never had a conversation with until I was an adult. I went on to have the most wonderful relationship with him for about six years before he died. I grew to love him deeply. I was never sure before whether I loved him or not.

I suppose the real test of my recovery was when both my parents died unexpectedly in the space of eight weeks, two and a half years ago. Again my friends came to my aid and were only too willing to help. I credit myself every day for the way I've handled most things but my parents deaths still hurt a lot. I've gotten so much from GROW that it goes without saying why I'm still an active member. I still get embarrassed when people tell me how good I am to have come through because the greatest compliment any of us that have been through the programme will get, is to see others making progress. We say in GROW that some day you will wear your breakdown as your badge of honour and I'm proud to wear mine.

Emer's Story

I came into GROW four years ago suffering from chronic anxiety and panic attacks. I found a lot of people to be unsympathetic with a 'snap out of it' attitude. I felt very isolated despite being surrounded by friends. There is, of course, an unspoken shame and sense of stigma about anything to do with nerves or mental collapse, so, for about five years I would suffer chronic nagging headaches, fatigue, weariness and loss of appetite. Always an ache or a pain, some unease and discomfort and then, with a full blown panic attack, the fear and the danger were so unbearable that my hands sweated , my mouth went dry, my head felt dizzy, my legs shaky and weak. I gripped things so tight that my knuckles turned white; feelings of terror and dejection with no warning bells; and inexplicable fear of something! I felt so alienated my world was gradually getting smaller as I feared the attacks; a feeling of well being was now a stranger to me!

I tried doctors and various medicines, but deep down I knew I had to do something more constructive. From the moment I entered GROW I knew I had found what I was looking for.

GROW, at first, seemed to open a can of worms as I started to look at my life. I'd had a very poor relationship with my parents; I was reared by my mother's sister and her husband. They only had one child, a son who was twenty years older than me. In many ways my upbringing was very privileged, especially with regard to material things, but something was lacking. I always knew my mother, father and six brothers and sisters, however, my situation caused me considerable pain and a lot of insecurity.

My life went on, I married young but life still had its ups and downs. There was plenty of joy and many sorrows; unemployment, emigration, my sister's illness and the death of my aunt, who reared me, after a long illness.

I also had a problem with my eldest son who has dyslexia. He is a very demanding child and his learning disability has caused me a lot of anxiety. However, I have learned to decentralize myself from him. I know now I can only desire his welfare but I cannot achieve it.

The first task the group gave me was to find time for myself and to 'settle for disorder in lesser things for the sake of order in greater things and therefore be content to be discontent in many things'. I also learned and gained a great understanding of feelings and a great insight into my condition. I learned how to say 'No', as 'Yes' means nothing if you don't know how to say no. I tried very hard to do my tasks and learn the program. I have a big idea of God; I have hope and I know 'people who matter don't mind and people who mind don't matter'. I'm 'not put off lovely things by objectionable people'.

I guess the most challenging thing I did since joining GROW was to visit my sister who was ill in California. There were so many obstacles in my way; the fear of a panic attack during the long flight with no escape. The fear of seeing my sister and also my mother who was there at the time. But I didn't let fear be my master and I made the trip which I found to be very healing in many ways, especially with relationships. The prayer in the red book Surrender Your Loved Ones helped me deal with my ill sister and her subsequent death, just after I returned home. I am grateful that I made the trip.

I feel now that I have learnt to value my self worth, respect and self esteem. That I'm in good shape to build a good relationship with others.

Since I became a fieldworker, I must say I'm really enjoying the job. I am still getting used to it. It's the kind of job where you get thrown in at the deep end, although I find people to be very helpful. I know I don't know it all and the learning and growth has to continue.

I know my essential function is to animate and inspire a caring and sharing community with the living spirit and the example of GROW friendship, and to activate the quality control of leadership and the Group Method of all the groups in my care.

I have a very busy life outside of GROW. Sometimes I find it difficult to get the right balance but I know in time this will come. At the moment I am working on dealing with my relationship with my mother, who is a very difficult person and has caused me a lot of hurt in the past. I'm trying to accept her for what she is and forgive. I know this will take time and my reading is The Affirmation of Good.

I enjoy life now, too much time is spent concentrating on past or future experiences. I try to enjoy each moment as it happens.

I can't say the changes I have made have been easy and I have fallen down a few times, but I always 'resume without fuss'. I use The Four Stabilising Questions all the time and The Three Basic Determinations, especially 'to go by what I know not by how I feel'.

I have to say I am coping well. My home life with my husband and three children is much calmer, co-operative and friendly. I put my trust in the 'Supreme Healer'; I remind myself that 'you alone can do it but you can't do it alone'. I don't blame anyone for what happened in my past; I live 'one day at a time'. I'm off all medication now and I no longer fear panic attacks; it must be over a year since I had one. My main supports for facing life now are 'my built in habits of personal maturity (understanding, acceptance, confidence, control and love). Not the doctor, nor the pills, nor even the group'. I am positively glad of what happened to me because it turned out to be a breakthrough to better and happier living and I know now that 'the best in life and love and happiness is ahead of me'.

Jean's Story

I joined GROW in 1981. I didn't know what was wrong with me. I knew nothing about mental illness and thought phobias were something people got and kept for the rest of their lives. I did know I was unhappy, bored and terrified of being left on my own. Five of my ten children had left home and the younger five were growing up fast. An obsessive thought went round and round in my head. I saw an empty future in which my children had all grown up and gone their own ways and Tom my husband, had died. I planned to kill myself when this happened rather than being alone. I had a vast collection of phobias - I couldn't sit in a dimly-lit room or a room with curtains drawn. I would panic in any crowded place and hasten to get away from cameras. My world was getting smaller and smaller and blacker and blacker.

It was my feeling of boredom that saved me. I knew I had to find an interest. I tried various things but they were all boring! Then I saw an advertisement for GROW. I didn't know what GROW was, but decided to give it a try. The impression I took home from my first meeting was somewhat confused - all these people holding hands in a circle - was it a seance? At least it wasn't boring so I'd try it again. I did - and again, and again ...

I liked the people in the group but, at first, the program was rubbish. I was given Personal Value to work on. This made no sense to me until, one day, I connected it up with My Three Vital Needs. I read them over and over and began to apply them to myself and I got a few insights.

'Unique Identity': I had no identity. I had spent thirty years at home. I had been labelled "wife", "mother", "housekeeper". When I sent a cheque to the bank or paid a bill, the receipt would invariably go to Tom at his place of work. Jean didn't exist.

'Personal Value': I had placed all my value on the fact that I was good at having babies. I hadn't been good at anything before that, and now I wouldn't be good at anything ever again. I had seen achievements as my only value and now I was useless.

'Security and Loving Harmony': No. I was desperately insecure. If Tom didn't arrive home at the expected time, I was certain he was either dead or out with another woman and I would be hysterical when he arrived. Not much harmony when he did turn up!

'Purpose and progress': the children were all very independent. They didn't need me any longer. Nobody needed me. If my only purpose in life was to cook and wash and iron for Tom - well, I didn't want it.

With the group's help, I worked on my vital needs. In the group I was "Jean". I had an identity at least. I worked on 'If anything is worth doing, it is worth doing badly - for a start, and while you're improving' and 'If in doubt whether to express a thing or not, express it'. The realisation that it was okay to do or say something imperfectly came as a great surprise and I worked on these pieces over and over. This was great. I didn't have to be perfect. I had always been terrified of making mistakes, being criticised, being laughed at. I had allowed this fear to stop me from doing a lot of things I wanted to do and from saying things I wanted to say.

Mutual help - 'The more maladjusted I am the more I need help, yet to grow out of maladjustment I need to become concerned for and helping others'. This aspect of Grow helped me a lot. It was great to realise that I could help others as they helped me. I wasn't quite useless after all. I didn't see it at the time but, even after that first meeting, I was decentralising - at home, I thought of the group members. These positive thoughts crowded out my unhealthy obsession about the future until, eventually, the present was all that mattered.

The Three Basic Convictions

1. I am not acting alone but cooperating with the invincible power of a loving God and with trustworthy and friendly helpers.

2. I can compel my muscles and limbs to act rightly in spite of my feelings.

3. My feelings will get better as my habits of thinking and acting get better and

The First Stabilising Question - 'What exactly am I troubled about?' used together worked really well. When I found it almost impossible to 'compel my muscles and limbs' I would ask myself 'what exactly am I troubled about?' I found that if I changed this bit and said "what am I afraid of?" it worked even better. I could see there was absolutely nothing to be afraid of. It was just a feeling, so I'd go ahead and do it. My feelings did get better as my habits of thinking and acting got better. I didn't have to work on my phobias directly.

Healthy Intention - 'I tend to defeat my own purpose when I aim primarily at enjoyment, health, approval, popularity, safety, salvation, holiness or happiness; or try too hard to achieve any of these. On the other hand I find that if in each case I strive for something more important that transcends me then the desirable thing in question tends to come my way as a result. I will therefore grow to mental, social, spiritual and physical health and happiness by consistently striving for a naturally wholesome and loving life with those about me under God's providence, this is for the kind of life which will make me capable and worthy of happiness.'

I was lucky the desirable things came my way as a result of growing in other areas of my life.

I took on leadership roles as they turned up. I became recorder five months after I had joined. I did group support. Became organiser a year later. Organised three different groups. Joined the Executive and, a year later, was elected National Chairperson. (If you want quick promotion, join GROW!). This was tough. It meant a lot of hard work. I studied GROW's Articles, Company Law and business books. It was a very slow process. Reading and writing are a real problem to me. My eyesight was damaged irrecoverably (as well as my face disfigured) in a traffic accident when I was 24 (yes cars did go that fast back in 1951!). With a lot of help from the Executive members, the Administrative Secretary and the Fieldworker as well as my group and the program I struggled on. I learnt a lot and grew a lot. When things went wrong - they often did - I found it a great consolation to tell myself I didn't have to be perfect or know everything. I just had to do my best and 'accept various faults as a natural part of my improving self'.

Currently my roles in GROW are many and varied. I enjoy it all and certainly am not bored. I 'settle for a lot of disorder in lesser things for the sake of order in greater things'. I work on Truth - 'Mental health is truth - the conformity of my mind with reality. It comes from thinking, speaking and living truly. A true response to each situation, to my human helpers and the Supreme Healer can and must be made at every stage of my recovery or personal growth'.

I am really pleased I found GROW when I did instead of getting into the psychiatric system or becoming dependent on medication. I took the "rough road" and am fully convinced it got me a lot further than the "smooth" one could have done. I would like to say "thanks" for the Programme and the Group Method as well as to all the friends I found in GROW for their unwavering and on-going help and support all the way.

Mary O's Story

The most terrifying aspect of depression for me was the feeling of help-lessness, the feeling that I was losing control and becoming a spectator of my own life.

I am the product of an extremely crushing, authoritarian culture - the Ireland of the forties and fifties. In my own family circumstances I was crushed further by poverty and alcoholism. Through these family cir-cumstances my education was cut short and I ended up in a job I de-tested. As far as I could see the only way out was to get married, which I did at twenty two, and had three children before I was twenty seven. I hardly know how I got through those years. I was so ill-prepared for bring-ing up a family. All I know is that I arrived into my forties having no idea of who I was, full of anger and not knowing exactly why, burdened with guilt about matters that had nothing to do with me, and an overwhelm-ing sadness that overshadowed my every waking hour, along with being in a constant state of dread and panic.

On top of all that my robust physical health was beginning to let me down and it was during a visit to the doctor with my physical ailments that I was prescribed medication for depression and sleeplessness. This was terrific for a time - to get a bit of ease from myself - but deep down I kept asking myself "surely this cannot be what life is about". I wanted to be more than what I was. I wanted to make my very best contribution to life. Instead I felt my life was all over and, on the other hand, I felt it hadn't begun. It was in this state of mind that I found myself, one freez-ing January night, in a GROW group in Liberty St., Cork. That was eleven years ago. I took to the group like a duck to water. I loved the structure and the discipline of the Group Method, the way it facilitated the group to be conducted in an orderly fashion, addressing all eventualities that can arise when a group of people sit down to hold a meeting.

The Problem Solving in the group was a real eye opener for me. Each problem was discussed and teased out in a rational, caring way. I had never learnt to deal with problems in this way. All my life I had, first of all, denied I had problems and, secondly, decisions that had to be made were made by how I felt, rarely going through the reasoning process. Consequently, I never had any real choices. Over the first couple of years I worked on most of the programme - Blue, Red and Brown Books. However, to accommodate the need to keep this testimony within a certain length, I have, after careful reflection, selected three programme pieces and three of the Twelve Steps that significantly helped me.

1. The Principle of Being Ordinary:

'I can be ordinary. I can do whatever ordinary good people do and avoid whatever ordinary good people avoid. My special abilities will develop in harmony only if my foremost aim is to be a good ordinary human being'. I had never seen myself in an ordinary light. I only saw myself as someone whose main function in life was to make other people happy. So, in order to achieve this, I set about trying to change people to the way I wanted them to be - HAPPY. I smile now when I think about my own ridiculous expectations of myself. I was basically playing God. You can imagine how much pressure went off me when I stopped that nonsense. This principle also promised me 'that my special abilities would develop in harmony only if my foremost aim was to be a good ordinary human being'. As I focused more on changing myself and developing myself, my special abilities naturally got better. I have achieved things in my life since practising this principle that I would never have thought possible. So, in fact, by becoming ordinary I became special. That's a bit of a paradox.

2. The Overall Key to Mental Health:

'There is one brief practical formula for mental health:

Settle for disorder in lesser things for the sake of order in greater things and therefore be content to be discontent in many things'. Through putting this programme piece into action I began, once again, to take back my power. My power to reason, my power to make a choice as to how I was going to react to a certain situation. Up until then I made no choice. I just went in with all guns firing. Consequently, I alienated others from me and detested myself for acting so out of control and immaturely. It's so terrific now to understand that whatever is going wrong it is certainly not more important than my relationships with others and my peace of mind.

3. Principle of Personal Value:

'No matter how bad my physical, mental or spiritual condition I am still a human person loved by God and a connecting link between persons. I am still valuable, my life has a purpose and I have my unique place and my unique part in God's work'. I believe that the whole GROW programme is designed and fashioned towards bringing to us the understanding and acceptance of basic truth, no matter what has happened, no matter what wrongs I have done, no matter how disordered my mind, I am still basically a valuable person - simply because I am a human being with a massive potential to achieve good. I have learnt through working on this principle that until I can accept myself and believe in my own goodness that I can never accept or find any good in the world around me. I am very pleased with the basic harmony that I am beginning to experience within myself as I truthfully assess my weaknesses and strengths.

Step 1: We admitted we were inadequate or maladjusted to life.

The more I go forward in my life, the more I challenge myself, the more I have to make this step because, as I step out and take on challenges, I need the help and advice of others, even if it's only to talk things out. When we come so far the danger is that we think we don't need help.

Step 8: We learnt to think by reason rather than by feelings and imagination.

As I am blessed with a fertile imagination, I have to work very hard to keep it in check. My feelings and imagination could override my reasoning abilities. However, when I get the three working in balance at times I get fairly good results.

Step10: We took our responsible and caring place in society.

I try my best to be true to myself. If I see things gong on around me that are not right I try to have the courage to do something about them. Sometimes though I fail because of my fears or lack of wisdom. I continue to work on this step. Another aspect of GROW that helped me enormously was being encouraged to take on leadership roles. Taking on these roles was intrinsically linked to my recovery and growth. I was an Organiser, Regional Chairperson, Executive Member and I am now the Fieldworker in the Cork/Kerry Region.

The friendship I found inGROW cemented all the other aspects of the programme together - real friends who challenged and believed in me - and supported me as I struggled to take on those challenges.

Having come out of an authoritarian culture, I had got into the habit of feeling I had to get other people's permission on everything I did, I seemed to be always looking over my shoulder, seeking other people's approval. It is a great freedom for me to understand that I can trust myself to do the right thing and that the only approval I need is my own. Consequently, I don't take myself too seriously any more. I know my own expectations of myself and I have a sense of humour about my failings most of the time. I don't have to meet other people's standards. This is a great freedom for me. When life is fired at me point blank nowadays I find I have the ammunition to fight back. I am not overpowered and destroyed by my helplessness. I enter into each day with hope and confidence and most of the time it turns out fine. Sometimes I arrive at the end of my day a little battle scarred but I can reason out that whatever has gone wrong is only another learning opportunity so that I can go forward to my goal which is to become all that I can be, so as to make the best possible contribution to life, which I so earnestly want to do.

Francis's Story

I was reared on a farm in the country, where I still live. At the age of 3 my brother of 7 years died. He was never very well, having been an invalid from birth and there was something wrong with his heart. I can still remember when I was upstairs with him, he was in one cot and I was in another. Every morning he would put out his hand to shake mine. I missed him a lot. His name was Sean.

I started school and got on fine. It was a two teacher school. I was in my last year in national school when my father got a heart attack. He died 2 days later in hospital. The whole family was devastated. My mother took it very badly as they were very close. I had three brothers and three sisters and an uncle living with us. After my father's death I became very withdrawn and found it very hard to mix with other children.

A few months later I started secondary school. It was in the next few years that my life went downhill. I was sexually abused by a teacher there for two years. That was from September 1972 to some time in 1974. There was no talk about sex abuse then like there is now. So I told no one about it. I felt dreadful at the time. I thought there must be something wrong with me that he was doing this. I felt ashamed and dirty and I was between the ages of 12 and 14.

I left school at the age of 16. I worked on the farm at home for a year. This was fine as I was meeting very few people and I preferred to isolate myself. I thought other pupils in the school knew what he was doing and that they were laughing at me behind my back. I worked hard and met as few people as I possibly could. I started working for my brother when he went out on his own building houses.

At the age of 19 I had my first breakdown. I felt very strange at the time. I felt I had a lot of power and kept praying and thinking something terrible would happen if I didn't. I felt under terrible pressure. When a door would open I would think it was someone coming to get me. I was admitted to Hospital and I was there for 6 weeks. I don't remember a lot of the first few weeks there, but I was very hard to manage. When I came home I was on a lot of drugs, so I was sleeping every chance I got. I was back in hospital many more times.

I felt it very strange that no one told me what was wrong with me. Then maybe this was the way psychiatric patients were treated. I asked my local doctor what was wrong with me. He said I was suffering from schizophrenia. It came as a big shock as I had often read about how violent people suffering from this can be and I had never been violent to anyone. I was admitted to hospital several times for many years. Sometimes I would be home only a few months when I would be back in again.

I attended an orientation meeting telling people about GROW This was the first I heard about GROW. I didn't go straight away but the more I thought about it the more I thought it could help me. I went to my first meeting in July of '91. That is over 4 years ago. I have met some wonderful people since then, like Sr. Brid who helped me to keep doing my practical tasks and to keep learning pieces from the blue book when I felt like giving up. She was there many a time I felt like giving up. I need only lift the phone and the sound of her voice alone would reassure me that things would be a lot better in the morning. Sr. Brid was a great friend to me and to GROW. She died of cancer in June of '94.

When I joined GROW I was suffering from anxiety, panic attacks and depression. When I would be doing certain jobs on the farm like washing the milking machine, which had to be done twice a day every day, I would get very anxious and have to leave the job there. I could not put up with the feeling inside me. So the first bit out of the Blue Book I was given to work on was one of the 3 Basic Convictions - 'I can compel my muscles and limbs to act rightly in spite of my feelings'. This helped me a lot. I went on to the 5 First Keys for Understanding Feelings. Pieces like these and others helped me back to thinking positive, that there was hope for me and that I was not a hopeless case with schizophrenia.

Personal Value kept me going as well - 'No matter how bad my physical, mental or spiritual condition I am still a human person, loved by God and a connecting link between persons; I am still valuable, my life has a purpose and I have my unique place and my unique part in God's work'. Through working on these and other parts of the Blue Book I started getting more confidence in myself and started meeting more people, not avoiding them as I used to before.

I worked hard on the program for the first year and seldom missed a meeting. I gained an awful lot from it. Looking back now on the way I was when I joined and the way I am now I have an awful lot to thank GROW for - for the programme and the members in it. I am looking forward to life now, not dreading what tomorrow will be like as I so often used to. I did a course on car maintenance, which was a result of a task I got. I also learned to swim, all through GROW.

Recently I started helping with an Orientation Group in the psychiatric hospital where I was a patient. This meant a lot to me as I was giving back some of the help I received. I am working on Acceptance and Confidence at the moment. I still have a bit to go before I could say I am fully recovered. But I will keep working on the GROW programme for as long as it takes.

Marianne's Story

My name is Marianne. I'm 39, married to Jim. We have four children. In my original family there are eight of us, I being the second eldest.

When I was young my parents looked on me as being weak and my having red hair seemed to confirm this for them. They were very superstitious and red-haired girls were to be avoided at all costs.

My mother came from a very proud, hard working, no nonsense farming family. My father was from the town. His father was very fond of drink and he often ill-treated his wife and children.

We lived with my aunt Brigid and her two daughters and she was quick to point out that it was her house and only for her we'd be on the road. She was a bully, often hitting us, seeming to care little for the feelings of those closest to her. When I was 9, after a row between Mammy and my aunt, we moved to my grandfather's house. He took an instant dislike to me, often calling me names and hitting me with his stick. My uncle lived there too. He was a bachelor and had little time or patience for children. So I feared my aunty, uncle and granda and for the very roof over my head. These fears and many more have stayed with me all my life.

Dad went to England to work when I was a baby. Often he did not work or send money. Mam used to borrow money from a neighbour or from aunt Brigid, who was very disapproving of such behaviour.

As a child I was criticised and made to feel a fool, as if I was in the way. I felt I was a nothing and a nobody. My father was away a lot and when he did come home he wasn't interested in work. He socialised, drank, stayed in bed and my mother was weighed down with problems, children, pregnancies, ten in all, an irresponsible husband, money problems and lack of help and support from my father. Neither of my parents tended to my emotional needs. They fed and clothed me as best they could but as regards feelings, they didn't want to hear about them.

I can never remember being told I was loved or wanted, I didn't feel special, I didn't get hugs. I was told I was good only when I helped out or worked very hard. Even then praise came in the form of criticism. I often heard "It's a pity you can't be good like that all the time" ringing in my ears. I tried harder and harder to please and be good. I didn't feel accepted for who or what I was. I only felt approved of and wanted when I was doing something for others.

As a person I felt no good, lazy, dirty, ugly, good for nothing and sometimes told that too. Mam blamed dad, as did granda, my uncle and aunt, for us not having money or a home of our own. I grew up listening to the people I lived and depended on criticising each other, us and everyone else and there were numerous rows. They either looked up to or down on people. I also developed this nasty habit.

I hated my father and I blamed him too and everything he said irritated me. I had a quick temper and I wasn't slow to tell him how I felt about him. So living in a family like that, yes, there were many happy times but also very many sad painful times. I didn't and couldn't allow myself to feel the pain then. So I buried it all. If I showed anger I was told it was wrong, nice girls don't act like that. If I cried and wanted comfort I was told to stop being a baby or to 'get up out of there you big lazy lump and do a bit of work'. I would have loved if someone could have put their arms around me but it didn't happen. At an early age I decided I didn't need love, hugs or gentleness so that I wouldn't feel disappointed and rejected when I didn't get any.

At 13 I experienced some sexual abuse. Looking back I can see I was trying to please the person involved. At 15 I took an overdose of tablets. I was studying for my Inter Cert and baby-sitting my brothers and sisters. The chaos was still going on in the house and I felt it was all too much. I had to go to hospital to be pumped out. Things didn't improve as a result, only got worse.

At 18 I began to get headaches. By now I was studying for my Leaving Cert.

I started work as a telephonist in 1973 and became friendly with a girl I trained with. She accepted me as I was and I warmed to this. When she was transferred to another county I missed her terribly. I couldn't cope with the parting and I started to attend a psychiatrist and was on medication for a short time.

I met my husband Jim in 1974 and we got engaged in 1975. Those few years were the happiest of my life. I was living away from home, had money and clothes and felt free.

In 1975 Mam was diagnosed as having cancer. This was a terrible blow. My father's escape was drink. The following years again became very difficult. I took on a lot of the workload and problems from home. My brother was involved in a serious car accident in 1977. Thank God he recovered.

Jim and I married under great stress in 1978. We'd had two years of mam's illness and hospitalisation, dad's constant bouts of drinking and my younger sisters and brother to be looked after. Mam died two months later. She was three weeks from her 50th birthday. My youngest sister was only 9. Again dad drank and neglected the younger children. He turned against Jim and me for a while. I was in the middle of minding and taking care of everyone. I neglected my own health and had a very stressful life. By this time I had lost touch with my feelings and I didn't know what my own needs were.

I had my first baby in 1981, followed by another in 1983, one in 1984 and the last in 1990. I suffered postnatal depression after each one and was depressed during my last two pregnancies. I had a Caesarean section with my third child. After my second child was born my doctor prescribed antidepressants. They helped a little.

After my third child I was prescribed more antidepressants and after a few weeks was referred to a psychiatrist. More tablets were prescribed: antidepressants, tranquillizers and sometimes sleeping tablets. I was on twelve tablets a day and not feeling much better. I was like a zombie on medication for 6 years.

During those years of black depression there seemed to be no light. I felt suicidal and wished I had the courage to take the box of tablets or go to the lake. Two things stopped me. The first was I didn't want to hurt Jim or the children and secondly if I lived I'd have to live with the consequences. I was cranky, bitchy, fearful constantly and worrying about everything. It took me all day to do my chores. I was unable to cope. I didn't want to go out, not even to town, and when I did go I felt I was in a bubble, separated from everyone else. I felt lost and frightened. If I saw someone I knew I crossed the road rather than speak to them. I felt isolated even when with people.

Jim used to come home early from work to help me. He is a plumber and we also work the farm. I was unable to relax or even sit for any length of time. I was always on the go. I was ashamed to tell anyone.

The stigma of depression and mental illness was with me in those days. I lost weight and had little interest in how I looked. Nobody knew of my suffering and I succeeded in keeping it secret. I compared myself unfavourably with others.

My children suffered also. Because I was so depressed I had little patience and took it out on them. I slapped them, sometimes with my hand or sometimes with a wooden spoon or stick. I roared and shouted at them and took all my feelings of anger, frustration and helplessness out on Jim and the children. I had vowed to myself that I would treat my children with love and respect and not bring them up the way I was reared. I was actually repeating the same process although I could not see that yet. Going to bed at night I felt I was a bad wife and mother. My feelings of guilt were extreme. I used to think if only someone would punish me I would be better and kinder. I tried hard to be gentle, kind and loving. It was like a heavy weight on me. Each night I prayed that tomorrow would be different, but it never was. I got to the stage where I hated going to bed at night because all too soon the morning would come and another dreary day of trying to cope with depression, three small children, holding on to the anger that was raging inside, when all I wanted was to be at peace and have a happy family life.

The psychiatrist advised me to go to GROW. I did so with reservations the following Monday night. Looking back I'm surprised I went. I was afraid anyone would speak to me. What would I say? I was shy and awkward with people and had no self-worth. The first time I was asked to read from the brown book it was like I could hear someone else reading, I was so nervous. I didn't understand a word I read. I soon discovered I could no longer just sit and think about my problems or blame others. The first piece I got out of the blue book was Responsibility. On reading it I wondered how anyone knew I was blaming my parents. My task for a long time was to take 10 minutes for my coffee break. I used to sit watching the clock until it was time to get up.

As a result of being brought up in a dysfunctional home, I was a perfectionist and a workaholic. I was unable to do all I was doing, but I kept pushing myself. I did my task religiously each week, read the blue book and rarely missed a meeting. It was my lifeline. I found the week long between meetings but the friendships within GROW extended to outside and without this I don't think I would have continued going. At long last I was being accepted and understood for who and what I was. There was a common bond and trust. Not only was I getting help, but I soon discovered that I could help others. This knowledge was as important to my health and growth as the help others gave to me. My next task was to go for a walk. I often didn't go until Sunday or Monday and I hated leaving the house, I found the Three Basic Determinations most helpful. Next I started to look at my relationship with Jim. The Companionship Test helped with this also Regard for Others. I was unable to laugh or be happy, unable to apologise when in the wrong or even to admit being wrong. I was very difficult to live with in those days. I began to see what it was like for Jim and the children.

Again the Blue book helped. I used Regard for others, Control and Bedrock. I didn't find the tasks easy and often didn't want to do them. Sometimes I went back to a meeting not having done the tasks at all.

After a few months in GROW I was asked to be organiser. This I didn't want to do and felt very frightened. I felt I wasn't good enough and wouldn't be able to do it properly. But in the end I decided to give it a go. Taking on the role of organiser has been an important step for me. I have learned to take on responsibility like opening up for the meeting, attending the Knock O & R meetings, dealing with correspondence. Little jobs for me today, but very big back then. The Three Basic Convictions helped.

It was around this time I began to experience migraine headaches. I've had hundreds more since. I would always feel stressed beforehand. Over the years I have tried everything to eliminate them. I've been to specialists and faithhealers, I've had bio-energy and Shen therapy, acupuncture and reflexology. Acupuncture helped most of all. My poor husband and children have been through hell and so have I. My doctor used to give me an injection of morphine, pethadine or voltoral when the headache was very bad.

For nine months I had injections every week. I've been on pain killers from mild to strong and also on preventative tablets. All to little avail. I used to get an upset tummy as well. I got sick so often, even today I find my tummy is easily upset. I used to get gastroenteritis at other times, which confined me to bed for a few days per week. My children at this time were aged 1, 2 and 4 years.

Over the years I've spent thousands of pounds on my ill-health. On GROW I've spent nothing and it has helped me to such an extent that I can now prevent a lot of my illness. I no longer have a gastric tummy, migraine I still get but less severe and I am rarely confined to bed. I don't always have to take tablets and only one injection in the last three years.

Patricia, a GROW member, was already in GROW when I joined and we have become friends, helping each other over the years. It was she who first suggested I try to reduce my tablets. I thought she was mad. I'd rather have walked through the town naked. Eventually I decided to take on the challenge. Twelve months later with the help of GROW and a friend there - who was the organiser before me and a community psychiatric nurse - I was off all medication.

'The object of treatment is the end of treatment' was the piece in the blue book I found helpful, also Don't Sabotage and 7 More Keys for Understanding Feelings. The psychiatrist told me I'd probably be on treatment for life and warned me not to have another baby. I wanted to have another child and three months later I was pregnant. This was one task I didn't find difficult. August '90 my youngest son was born . Again I had depression during and after the birth. Although I went back to the psychiatrist he didn't prescribe medication. I didn't feel great and although I was coping better than before it wasn't easy. GROW meetings weren't being held in my local town at this time and I really missed them but I had learned a lot in the previous years and I understood more about depression. I had good friends to see me through and I used the GROW way as much as I could.

Three years ago my father died from a massive heart attack on the way home from the pub. He fell inside the ditch and was found 3 days later by a child going to school. He was 63. I was glad in a way that he was dead. I thought that problem would be out of the way. I didn't think I'd miss him, but I did. Shortly afterwards my health began to suffer again and I felt an unease all the time.

Three years ago GROW was restarted in my area and has moved from strength to strength. We now have 16 members.

A year and a half ago Jim and I decided to seek help with a sexual problem and we started to attend a counsellor. Her name is Teresa. After a few months I discovered my problem was related to my childhood and in June '93 started one to one counselling with Teresa. Somehow I was getting daddy and Jim mixed up in my mind. It got to the stage where I didn't want him to touch me. Here was the man I loved and I hated daddy. I was very mixed up.

GROW had helped me get my thinking straight. I was communicating better with most people and my relationship with Jim and the children had improved. I had confidence and had gained some self-worth. I had built up my personal resources and without all this I couldn't have faced into counselling.

As a child it was unsafe to feel. I became a thinking person. It was too painful to feel any emotions. During counselling I got in touch with all those buried feelings and emotions that were there since childhood. It has been a very tough and painful 2 years. I discovered that all the depression, migraines, tummy upsets and sexual problems were a result of my damaged upbringing, but today I have dealt with much of the past. I've worked at and succeeded in clearing away hate, blame, anger, resentments, revenge that were inside me. Recently I started to read the brown book again and it makes so much more sense to me now than before I had counselling. In particular step 4: Your Key to a Better Life, step 5: Is it healthy to feel guilt? and Responsibility, step 8: Distorted Thinking and Objectivity and step 10: Emotional Blackmail and Approach to Love. If I can live my life by it I'll be on the pig's back as we say in the West.

Today I've developed a more positive attitude. I'm caring, loving, gentle and kind. I have empathy with and compassion for people. I still feel sad, angry and resentful at times. I do and say things that hurt people, but I'm quick to say sorry. I try to accept myself as I am. I'm not perfect and not a saint. I try to love myself as best I can and everyone else too.

Jim used to say I was as stubborn as a mule. On hearing this I was very much on the defensive, accusing him of being insensitive and often went into sulky silences for days followed by more accusations.

I had to feel I was right in everything. Anything less than perfect wasn't acceptable to me and I would feel a failure and no good. So rather than accept criticism I flew into a rage and accused the other person instead. In this way I didn't have to accept my faults. I used to feel that people were always criticising me. If I thought others were doing better than me or were more intelligent, I found fault with them and felt jealous of their success. I could only see my own faults and the only way I felt good about myself was to try to knock others.

All the time I felt persecuted and very much the victim. When I was criticised, I felt it was criticism of me as a person, not my behaviour. Today I can separate the two. I know I'm a good person, but sometimes my behaviour is unacceptable and needs to be changed. Disturbed Thought and Personal Thought helped me to see what was going on.

I have learned to praise my children, to stop running them down and finding fault. I had so much anger inside me, anger at a lost childhood, at being an adult child and a childish adult, anger at not being accepted or understood and I took all this out on Jim and the children. I feel very sorry now, but I know I was doing my best at the time.

I still don't do things right all the time and I expect I never will, but I do try to see the good in others, in myself and in every situation.

Growing up and in the early years of my marriage I was a very dependent person. I was always an extension of someone else, especially in my relationship with Jim. Not being a person independent of others I didn't trust my own thoughts, feelings or opinions. I always thought Jim was right. Today I can see clearly that neither of us is always right or wrong, we are just different. We still have arguments as we don't always see eye to eye, but we are better able to compromise. Not only have I grown, Jim has too. He is not so rigid or self-righteous as he was. I used to take all the blame for any disagreements we had. I don't anymore. Page 27 in the blue book Reasonableness has helped me with this one.

Jim and I love each other very much and where once I felt in his shadow I now feel very much his equal. In Dec. '92 when I started to see Teresa, I didn't know who I was. I knew I was Jim's wife, my children's mother, my parents daughter and a sister to my family. I was a friend, but I really had lost all sense of myself, my thoughts, feelings, desires, opinions. I had begun to speak, think and act as I thought others wanted me to. I didn't know what I wanted or needed. I portrayed a false self to Jim, my family and everyone else. Without counselling I was unable to find or even know myself as a separate identity. Today Oct. '96, I can honestly say I've found what I've been looking and searching for. I know what I want out of life and I know what my needs are. I have opinions and for the most part can express them. I am in touch with my feelings, thoughts and desires. I actually like and love the real me, faults and all. I'm proud of myself, of my courage and achievements. Every now and then I give myself a clap on the back and say: "Yahoo, fairdos to you, old girl!" I don't mean to boast. I'm just very happy to have reached the stage I'm at.

For years I ran from the pain. I didn't want to face it. I didn't want to change. Through GROW I began to face and change my unacceptable behaviour and warped thinking. GROW too has enabled me to find and deal with the deeper pain. Last year I decided I had run long enough. I was ready to face that pain, I was no longer afraid. Today thank God I can meet pain head-on whilst at the same time being a wife, mother, friend and most of all myself.

So to GROW and all my friends I say a big thank you. In particular I'd like to thank my dear loving, patient husband Jim. Through thick and thin he has been there, I love him dearly... He is a great man and only for his strength I don't think I'd have the will to keep going. My children are young, but nevertheless I'm grateful to them. They have suffered too and in their own way they have helped me.

I can't say I've enjoyed the suffering and pain and I'm sure Jim didn't either, but together we've gotten through. We have a great relationship today and I can honestly say I'm glad I had a breakdown. I thank God in his wisdom for all the difficult, sad and painful times and for all the goodness in my life. I've been blessed indeed. I'm still working on my-self. At the moment I'm still trying to slow down. The Overall Key to Mental Health helps with this, also Let go and let God.

I do not blame my parents or relations any more. I've forgiven them all. They too have suffered. I know they did the best they could. I love them all.

It's four years since I wrote this testimony. My aunt died in Nov. R.I.P., I miss her and I can now see she was like a second mother to me. I used to think she was a bully and didn't care for others. She too was doing the best she could. She had a hard life, yet she always gave of herself, in loving me through her courage and strength. I'm going to GROW and still attending a counsellor. It's painful at times, but I'm happy to be getting to know myself at a deep level. GROW meetings are part of my life.

God. I love you all.

It's four months since I wrote this testimony. My aunt died in Nov. R.I.P. I miss her and I can now see she was like a second mother to me. I used to think she was a bully and didn't care for others. She too was doing the best she could. She had a hard life, yet she always gave of herself, in loving me through her courage and strength. I'm going to GROW and still attending a counsellor. It's painful at times, but I'm happy to be getting to know myself at a deep level. GROW meetings are part of my life.

The national weekend in Kerdiffstown was a weekend not to forget. I met many GROWers from around Ireland. There were excellent speakers in for the weekend too. The camaraderie and spirit of GROW was felt by everyone.

I made new friends, one in particular - Mary. We have kept in touch since and her friendship, care and kindness have cushioned some difficult times I've experienced recently.

GROW is made up of people like Mary, each at a different stage of recovery, showing bravery, courage and strength and at the same time they have the ability to reach out and help others in need.

Once again God has shone His light on me. My life has been enriched by having GROW.

My love to Mary and all GROWers,

Fran's Story

My name is Fran. To me growing is all about changing and I want to tell you a little about how GROW has helped me to change into the new me, the me who is reasonably well able to cope with life.

About 20 years ago, I was told that there was no hope for me. I would have to spend the rest of my life on tablets and would need frequent hospitalisations, because I was mentally ill. Over the years I was given labels of postpuerperal depression, schizophrenia and finally manic depression.

Looking back I can see how GROW has been able to guide me through a very difficult and painful period of having to change from a very self-centred and pretty useless individual to a useful person in a reality I had been trying to ignore before joining GROW.

My life before my first hospitalisation had been an isolated one, probably not obvious to people I knew, but I was basically a loner, a dreamer, without any responsibilities or commitments. I was part of a great number of people who confused freedom with doing what you like and everyone spent their time and energy looking for a good time.

I had started to study French at university but as my life at that stage was very much lacking in discipline, I found myself unable to study and spending more and more time in the pubs listening to loud music and trying to forget about reality. The reality of my life was that I was continually letting myself down by not doing any study and I tried to avoid the tension this created by moving away into what was known as the sub culture.

My home situation had been far from peaceful and was certainly not conducive to study. I started staying out after school and hanging around coffee bars because of a fear of my stepfather's violent outbursts. He was deaf and unable to relate to anyone in the family which often resulted in unbearable tension. After finishing secondary school I moved out to a university town because I had been given a grant to study, but I was in no way able for the amount of study I was expected to do. I spent a lot of time daydreaming. I didn't like being alone in my flat and preferred the environment of the pub, the loud music and the proximity of people whose faces I knew, even though I didn't really know any of them. I had only one real relationship, a girl friend I could talk to and hitch hiked around with, looking for excitement. I was leaving myself wide open to abuse and my life, since I was about 13 until I got married, had been a story of sexual harassment and attempted rape at almost regular inter-vals. I was completely unable to accept my own and other people's sexu-ality. I was trying to ignore or suppress sexual feelings for so long that they kept cropping up at times when I didn't want them to, but I didn't know what to do with them and they became almost like an outside force that was stronger than me.

One night at a party I decided to set off for India on a bike. Looking back I believe it was an attempt to escape from an unacceptable reality into a spiritual world. I had been given a book by my real father entitled "The Life and Teaching of the Masters of the Far East" describing the life of yogis who "had overcome the world". When I set out I brought only a change of clothes with me. I cycled to Munich and from there on con-tinued teaming up with different people on the road to India. I spent the next three years or so travelling from place to place. On one of these journeys I met Mike, who I was later to marry, but at this stage I had a very warped idea about men. The only way that I could accept men was as "spiritual brothers" and the idea of being a sexually attractive woman was totally unacceptable, if not repulsive to me. So for more than a year we lived in a completely unnatural situation, living in the same quarters in a yoga school, often sharing the same hotel room or other sleeping accommodation and trying desperately to ignore or suppress any sexual overtones. When an Indian priest, a friend of ours, pointed out how un-natural and unhealthy this way of life was, I made a commitment in my head, in cold reason, that I would belong to Mike. The reality of this decision was more difficult. As I had suppressed any sexual feelings for so long, I was unable to respond in an emotional way to any advances made by Mike over quite a number of years.

The next part of my life story finds us in Ireland, in a very remote cottage in Clare, with no water or electricity. In my head everything was ideal, there were no problems with the pregnancy, but once the baby was born, the reality of having to cope with a baby and a husband, neither of whom I was sure I wanted or loved, hit me.

I don't remember much of what happened during my first nervous breakdown, but I remember having experiences that were totally "out of time". They had nothing to do with the reality of trying to recover from childbirth and preparing to go home and look after a newborn baby. They had mostly religious overtones: I remember thinking it was the first day of creation and running into the chapel in my pyjamas and sobbing that I was sorry for my sins.

After coming home from the mental hospital, I tried to carry on as best I could, but I had two more babies in the next three years and was totally unable to cope. I had regular stays in the mental hospital for the five or six years after my first nervous breakdown and I had tried hard enough, but it was really like trying to fit a square peg into a round hole. I never felt at home and I was always dreaming about the past and the reality I had known and I felt like I had been just physically lifted out of my own environment and planted in a foreign and totally alien environment in which I had no part. Every so often things got too much and I exploded in a mad rage of anger and frustration.

Somehow in the middle, we stumbled on the GROW organisation. It was a last straw, as our reality kept on crumbling and there was less and less of a common reality to hold on to.

At that time I must have had more labels than most, one of which was that of a manic depressive. My relationship with the GROW meeting and the people in it was certainly a manic depressive one. One week I'd be in heaven, the next, I wouldn't be able to stay in the same room. I hated it. Mike had an impossible job trying to coax, bribe and threaten me into keeping going.

At the time, I had no idea of an outside reality. I was locked into my own world which was made up of an overpowering range of emotions, which I was unable to look beyond.

After nine months of trying to just be physically present at the GROW meetings, it dawned on me that people who had jobs and led organised lives must, in some way, be able to control or ignore their emotions to be able to do so. In relation to that I was given, as a practical task from the GROW book, the 9th of the 12 Keys for Understanding Feelings. It states how 'it is not simply a matter of being for or against feelings', how 'everybody goes by feelings of some kind or other'. What I understood or rather what was beginning to dawn on me, was that we could learn to distinguish between feelings, and then learn to cultivate, positive feelings and suppress negative ones. Actually this particular piece of the programme wasn't very easy to read or understand, but the final sentence was straightforward enough and it reads: 'If I really understand and care for the true values of life, I will always have more important things to care about than how I feel'. That was really the first thing that made an impression on me and from then on I was able to begin what must have been a change of thinking. It was the first time it dawned on me that I was different from other people, probably the first time I realised I had a problem! I was given a practical task to help me to get some beginning of order back into my home life. As my life (and energy) seemed to be controlled by my emotions, I was in the habit of burning myself out during the times that I felt energetic and totally collapsing in a heap when I felt that I had no energy at all. This was a very soul-destroying habit, as no matter how hard I worked when I was on an "up" swing, it would all be totally undone by the inevitable downs and I would have to start right back at the beginning. So my change of acting began when I had to try and consistently do one particular job - in my case the washing up - regardless of what else was done or wasn't done and keep that as an ongoing practical task over a long period of time. It's amazing how long it took to change my way of dealing with this one job. Sometimes I had to sit down in the middle of it and try to control my anger which I was in the habit of taking out on the crockery and anything else breakable that was within my reach at these times. I had to tell myself it was only a 10-15 minute job I was dealing with and not something that even deserved that kind of emotional outburst.

Once I mastered that one job, the rest of my life since then has been an extension of that same task which really was putting The Three Practical Points for Control into practice:

' 1. Never say I can't, if the thing in question is an ordinary and a good thing.

Do the ordinary thing you fear, do the ordinary that repels you.

2. When the time to keep a resolution has come, don't examine any more the pros and cons, just do it.

3. Remember that free wills become strong wills, only through acquired habits

- that is: the repetition of many acts, and time.

Sow an act and reap a habit.

Sow a habit and reap a character.

Sow a character and reap a destiny.'

I must say that these sentences at times were like a magic formula, they got me moving. I've come a long way since then, but I find I have to apply the same principle for every new thing I have to tackle: don't over-react, remember it is a good and ordinary thing to do and don't drama-tise the situation.

I have used the same pieces of the programme to tackle other jobs which I strongly felt I couldn't do, like getting up out of bed in the morning, joining social clubs, learning to drive. When I passed my driving test it really helped me to feel that I was regaining control of my life. It was successes like this that made the struggle worthwhile, even though every new challenge brought on renewed anxiety and fear of failure.

I think that I can say that I have worked really hard to change my ways of thinking and acting, and I still am. One aspect of the changes I have made during my life has been coming to terms with

I have been on medication for over 15 years since my first nervous breakdown which is now about 23 years ago. After a couple of years of mental illness, I was firmly convinced that the psychiatrist was very like God, that he could understand my state of mind before I uttered a word, and that he knew my thoughts better than I did. So I was in the habit of blurting out whatever my emotional state inspired me to say and treat-ing the psychiatrist as though he was an ally - he knew what I was talking about already and he would know what was the right thing to do in my situation. So I was really handing over control of my life to someone who I believed knew or would know more about my life than I did. So I needed to change my relationship with the psychiatrist and the same thing is true to say about the medication. I had to learn not to depend on my medication to sort out my feelings for me. I was completely ruled by my emotions, yet my task was to build up my life without paying heed to my unruly feelings. I had to try and forget about how I felt and about tablets and get on with my life as best I could.

I have learned through experience that unless I am working on changing my personal life, it is very little use to try and get off my medication. I don't believe medication (or no medication) should be an end in itself. It is madness to think anybody could feel good for however long a period and depend on that for survival. Unless we learn to tackle and counteract our feelings of depression and fear in a positive and courageous way and build up solid habits of confidence in facing difficult and painful situations, we can't honestly say we have left our need for tablets behind. Real good feeling comes from achieving good things, making efforts and enjoying the reward.

If we do, we'll learn the valuable and necessary lesson that there are no short-cuts in life and that the only way to come to terms with life is a painful and determined effort to deal with life in the way that the GROW programme is trying to teach us, to strive for maturity with the help of others and to use our common experience as a way to deal with the difficulties of life and to never give up trying.

To finish up I can tell you that after having had serious mental problems after the birth of our three children, and having been advised not to have any more children, it was quite a shock to learn that I was pregnant again after eleven years. I had to stop taking my medication while I was pregnant, but both my doctor and the psychiatrist I was attending, insisted that I would have to get back on it the minute the baby was born. I didn't have an easy time and I was expecting to have to spend yet another part of my life in the mental hospital, but I was surprised with how I was able to manage to keep going from one day to the next.

I went to see the psychiatrist every six or eight weeks and was able to build up a more realistic relationship. I told him how I was coping with difficult situations and after about a year he agreed to gradually reduce the medication.

Even after I was off the medication I kept going in to give the psychiatrist my report on progress. Then, even though I had to take the responsibility for maybe having a relapse or another nervous breakdown myself, I left the psychiatric care with the blessing of the psychiatrist.

Our youngest child will be nine years old this Christmas and because of my changed attitude to life, I've actually been able to enjoy her and I feel very grateful to the GROW movement for having made it possible for me. The fact that it has been possible to change, not only to survive but to come out of the terrible experience of mental breakdown a stronger and wiser me is still proving a great source of wonder to me and I hope I will never take being able to cope with life for granted.

Mike's Story

My name is Mike. My overriding memories of childhood are memories of freedom. A great gang of village boys and girls roaming the countryside, climbing trees, jumping streams, the world a safe and magical adventure. My parents were medical missionaries just back from Africa. Home was somewhere you went out from to savour and enjoy. I still don't know what went wrong with me. I was severely injured in a car accident and one theory is that I suffered brain damage. I have never gone along with that.

At 14 I was sent away to boarding school. I had been extremely bright early on at school but around twelve (which was around the time of my accident) everything began to go haywire. I didn't like being at boarding school and used the four years there to cultivate isolation, resentment and fantasy. I think a lot of me stopped living in the real world. I cut myself off from people and very much developed an "us and them" mind set.

When I left school I was very alienated. I had failed my exams and had no idea of what I wanted to do or be. I didn't want to be anything respectable. I worked for a year on a pig farm. I began to fantasise about being the prodigal son. I had begun to develop a crippling shyness. Things like speaking to someone or going into a room where there were people were terribly hard. I also found it nearly impossible to form an ongoing relationship with a girl and always seemed to be getting hurt. This in turn set up tormenting doubts about my sexuality and 'manliness'. For a few years I did things for about a year (a job or college) and then moved on. I was extremely passive but once or twice was shaken by a terrible anger that I glimpsed inside.

I was left some money so decided to travel. I hitched to India. I had the idea that I would go to Australia. After 8 months on the road I was in a very bad state. My thinking had become very peculiar. I developed a theory about eye colour. People with blue eyes came from the sky. People with brown eyes from the earth. I couldn't fit green eyed people in at all. I read the Bible a lot and one night read a passage where it warned about someone whose eyebrows met in the middle. This was a sign that someone couldn't be trusted. I looked in the mirror and found a few hairs in between my own. Another time I heard a distinct and menacing voice saying "We are going to get you!" and often noises in the street would turn into angry mobs trying to get at me in my hotel room. I ended up in a hippie colony in Goa. I thought I had a mission to get everyone off drugs and onto drink and remember leading a group into neighbouring Panjim to convert the mayor. I didn't sleep for a week. Every time I tried to go to sleep I thought I was going to die. It was as if my body was turning feet first upwards. I began to terrify myself with poetry that came from nowhere and thought I had to die young because the good do, although I thought I was evil.

I flew back to England and saw a psychiatrist. It was in a teaching hospital and I was asked if I minded if students sat in on the interview. I said no but I did mind. I was terrified of people but I didn't know how to say this. The doctor told me if I thought I was going mad then I probably was going mad. I had thought I must be sane because I knew a lot of my thinking and the way I behaved were mad. It was helpful to be told this truth.

I drifted on just able to cope, relying very heavily on drink, soft drugs and travel. I had been prescribed Librium. I started a business selling antiques from the east. On a trip to Afghanistan I met Fran who was to become my wife.

This was a huge turning point for me. I had a reason for being. I wanted to live. We went and studied Yoga in India and I got physically well. We married and moved to the West of Ireland. We bought a farm in a place called "Shean" or the "River of the Fairies". It was to be a new beginning. We would leave the world behind and find happiness.

When our first son, Tom, was born Fran had a very severe breakdown. I couldn't cope with it at all. I brought her home against the doctor's advice and had the most terrifying night of my life as Fran screamed that she was in hell and banged her head on the bare stone walls. She thought

Tom was Jesus and she had to give him to an old man who lived down the road because he had a picture of Our Lady on the wall. Next day I signed her in to the local psychiatric hospital.

Later I had to sign forms for shock treatment. Both were like experiences of dieing.

For three and a half years we struggled on. Fran was in and out of hospital. We became Catholics because we wanted to be full members of the local community. We had three lovely children in quick succession and were very mixed up about things like contraception. There were no young people around that we knew to talk to and of course both our families were miles away. I think I coped by working. I was the person who could do anything. I was milking 14 cows by hand and doing a lot of work for the neighbours as well as my own. I often had the 3 children propped up on the wall in the cow cabin while I milked as Fran would be in hospital. When she was out we tried lots of things to see would they help. Both of us thought that one day we would wake up and everything would be alright. We started the Co Workers of Mother Teresa, joined the charismatic renewal. One strange thing that happened when Fran became sick was that I was promoted to being well.

I just didn't know how to deal with Fran. One doctor would tell me I was too soft on her, the next that I was too hard. I was advised to join the Schizophrenia Association of Ireland and went to its first AGM. A lot of people had said they thought I was schizophrenic and maybe this experience helped me to keep on believing that inside Fran was a beautiful normal human being striving to get out.

In 1976 we found GROW. It was the first place where we found real hope. I had been left on the farm on my own for two weeks while Fran and our three children went on holiday to a convent. It was a really low point for me. I thought she would either commit suicide or go back to Holland or disappear into the hospital for good.

I spent the first year in GROW stuffing the programme into Fran. I was so bad that at one point I had to be asked to leave the room when she was asked how her task had gone. I was so insecure and raw that I always answered for her in case she said the wrong thing. The whole week would be geared to getting Fran to the next meeting. I remember nights when she would try and get out of the car while we were driving at 50 or 60 miles an hour. Other weeks she would be in bed the whole week and I would try to bribe her. The journey to GROW was a round trip of 65 miles and we never missed once. One night Joannie Baines attended the meeting from Australia. She had been diagnosed as schizophrenic and had recovered. She gave Fran a signed copy of her story and on it she wrote "If you keep coming to the meetings and doing what you are asked, you will begin to get better." That was a turning point for Fran.

After about a year I began to get onto the programme myself. The biggest step for me was to publicly admit that there was something wrong with me. I felt that if I admitted to being anything less than perfect then my whole world would crumble. I actually thought something would happen to me physically. That I would disappear or crumble into little pieces. It was a great relief to be allowed to see myself as just another 'inadequate and maladjusted human being' especially one who was 'loved by God' and by this group of people who were there for me every week. How I needed to be loved and to know that I was lovable. For me the meetings were tangibly healing. I was like a leper. Untouchable. I can still feel the pats on the back, the hugs after the meeting, the arms round my shoulders. I lapped them up like a dog starved of affection although my whole body would stiffen at any physical contact. I began to take on tasks. Some were hard, others easy. I realised through the programme that I was totally 'overcontrolled' when it came to feelings. I had spent years cultivating the ability to ignore my feelings and get through each crisis. I slowly worked on loosening up. I got tasks like saying hello to people, lifting my head when I became trapped with it down, imagining the world was looking at me. I had been told I was pathologically shy by a doctor, which to me meant I had no control over my shyness, now I was told to 'be ordinary', to 'go by what I knew, not by how I felt'. It worked. Our neighbours in Clare were terrific. Their life style included a lot of fun and a deep sense and practice of the spiritual. I went to a dance at an A.A. (alcoholics anonymous) function and found I could dance if Fran kept up a steady 'one two three, one two three' while we spun around the room.

Being asked to take on a leadership role had a profound effect on me. I had built up a consuming distrust of leadership, confusing it with power and manipulation. I began to change my thinking when I realised that to have a meeting someone had to chair it and that sometimes that person must be me. I was way out of tune with my expectations of others. I thought that if I challenged anyone in the meeting about irrelevant talk or even if I disagreed with something trivial they might have said, that they would get "violently" angry or be "incredibly" hurt. Of course they just said a simple "sorry" or even thanked me for telling them. I think I was 'giving too much importance to (what I thought would be) others feelings' as well as my own. That was very healing. I began to become a part of GROW and the community. I joined the parish committee. That was very difficult because I used to be most uncomfortable during all the meetings but the group kept me going and as I did, my confidence grew. I learned I didn't have to feel good about it and that 'confidence is very much an attitude of mind', that what I was doing was both 'good and ordinary'.

A big challenge came when Joannie Baines, on a second visit to Ireland, advised us to move from the farm. I had asked a lot of people if they thought we should move and everyone said that people break down just as much in the town as in the country. This was true but Joannie said that our home was like being in solitary confinement for Fran and that what she needed more than anything was involvement with people. So we moved. This was the low point of our whole recovery. This time instead of going into hospital because she was depressed Fran became as high as a kite. I couldn't get her admitted to hospital. It took a week during which time neither of us slept. Fran was a spiralling tornado of ever increasing irrationality, humour then anger, violence and despair. I will never forget our three small children sitting on the stairs as all our possessions sailed over their heads one night. They were as terrified as was I. Nights were awful. Fran would ask for water. I would get water. Fran would throw the water all over me or the bed. I would remonstrate, Fran would be sorry, then she would get angry and smash whatever was near. I would try and calm her and the most horrific moans would well up inside her. Then she would ask for water......

When she did finally go into hospital she was so confused that she hit a nurse who she thought was harassing another patient. I witnessed her being manhandled into a locked ward. The locked wards to me looked like pure hell. I lost faith in God and in GROW. I went to complain to a friend who happened to be a nun who had been a part of the group. Instead of complaining I cried... and cried. I think it was the first time I ever really cried in my life. The same thing happened next day. I went to complain to Miss Brown the Matron. She was a tiny, very kind woman. Again my complaints came out as big sobbing tears. She was very comforting. The group really helped me now. They challenged me "to seek the good". To learn to relax and work on myself. To allow Fran to go through what she had to go through. The Three Basic Determinations and the Keys for Understanding Feelings were my every breath.

Around this time we decided that I would go back to college to study psychology. I had an interview and was accepted.

We moved to Galway. I hired a van, stuffed the kids and all our belongings into it and picked Fran up from the locked ward. This ward had now become a regular feature of her stays in hospital. She was never again to be an in-patient.

In Galway we attended separate groups. I studied Arts and then psychology. I had a circle of friends. I was 35 they were 18. It was very healing. I got honours in everything. I went to the professor to ask if it could be a fluke. I volunteered the kids for every test going in the psychology department because I wanted to know they were OK.

One task we got was actually suggested by a psychologist who we both attended. We both had a problem with anger. Whenever we tried to discuss the kids or the future Fran would always get angry and I was always afraid of her anger. The task was to talk every night for a half an hour. Fran had to try different ways to control her anger. I had to find ways to give her space to do that, and indeed to find ways to overcome my fear and sense of helplessness. In this way anger became the problem instead of Fran and me. At one time we went for Marriage Guidance which we both found helpful. Fran said it was the first place outside GROW where she felt she wasn't seen as the one with mental problems. We were treated equally.

In 1983 I passed all my exams and began working for GROW. I found that studying psychology increased my belief in the GROW programme. All the good bits in psychology seemed to be in there as well, cognitive psychology, developmental psychology, vocational psychology. We moved yet again. I learned recently from my eldest son how hard for them the moving was.

I have found working for GROW very challenging. I have had to change an awful lot. I had to admit to attitudes that were really destructive and slowly work at changing them. This is slow and difficult. I am now able for most things, from giving public talks to singing songs, to writing articles. I have many, many hobbies. I paint, I love my garden, I swim, walk, read, write. I have many friends and life is good.

In 1987 we discovered a new baby was on the way. That was beautiful. Lizzie acted as focal point for the whole family. She really drew us all together.

In 1990 I began a Master's degree in Family Therapy. The course was extremely hard and it meant being away from home one night a week. Fran supported me in doing this which she has always done. There were four psychiatrists on the course. I met them as fellow students not as people with power over me. The course content again complimented and enriched my understanding of GROW.

I have made many mistakes in my life as an individual, as a child, as a spouse and as a parent. But I am at this stage well able to 'be content to be discontent in many things' because the important things are going in the right direction. Through GROW I met many people who helped me in very real ways. Often they helped me to work on other relationships. They have acted as another self giving me new ways to see things. I am proud of my home and my family. Our four children are fine young peopl. I find the prospect of the future very exciting but in many ways sobering as I realise more and more that the future belongs to us. We have to take responsibility for it so what I do is important and I realise how limited I am. I can see many problems ahead for all of us as human beings. I want to grow spiritually and in community. I would like to thank both Fran's family and my own who both remained friendly and supportive though far away and our neighbours in Clare and Galway. I would also like to thank Fran for being such a great soul mate through all our perambulations. I suppose my greatest realisation or belief is that we are not acting alone, but cooperating with a loving God and all we have to do is to keep on trying.

Rose's Story

I came to GROW in October 1975 and my life has changed dramatically since. Before I had heard of GROW I had spent 15 years attending psychiatrists. I did not believe that GROW or anyone could help me, but I was willing to try anything.

About 1960 I first started feeling physically ill. Pains in my chest etc. X-Rays showed nothing serious. I spent three weeks in hospital for a rest. The doctor at that time said he had not known anyone so young to be so physically worn out, and if I kept going at the rate I was going, then it would not be long until I would be mentally worn out. (A lot of rot, I thought).

I was always a very anxious person, but was able to cope. I didn't have any problems with my work and on the whole I got along very well with people. I was popular with my friends.

In 1961 I first visited a psychiatrist. By this time I was very ill physically, but the doctor couldn't find anything wrong. I was advised to see a psychiatrist, which I did. He prescribed Valium and sleeping tablets. I was never really well after that, and I had to see the doctor frequently.

Valium, Melleril, Stelazine, Largactil, Stemetil, Tryptonal, Laroxyl, Surmontil, Mogadon, Deloxine-Co, Pentone are some of the tablets I was taking. I had E.C.T. many times (at least 200) and spent much time in hospital, particularly in the last five years before coming to GROW.

My problems

I was convinced that people were always talking about me. I began to feel inadequate, inferior, useless, and hopeless. I couldn't cope, was frustrated, had no personal value. I became very difficult to get along with. Deep depression followed. All sorts of fears took possession of me. Fear of being alone, fear of dying, fear of some dreadful thing happening to me.

I thought people were in the walls of my room talking to me, but worst of all, listening to me and watching everything I did. To say I was terrified was putting it mildly. I heard "Little Green Men" (as I called them) calling me and I felt compelled to follow them. Often I would wake at night, pulling and tearing at the bed clothes and talking to invisible people. I felt dead bodies all around me at night. These were the "people" in the ceiling that I was communicating with and I felt that if I went to sleep they would come down and take possession of me - therefore I was frightened of going to sleep, though at the same time I was taking sleeping tablets.

Even worse than the depression was the terrible guilt I felt. I felt guilty about everything - if the weather was bad, if an accident happened to someone I didn't even know. It nearly drove me mad when my relative got rheumatic fever. I thought it shouldn't have happened to him, I should have got it.

When deeply depressed nothing seemed to matter. I was just as happy to be sad and depressed as I was to be happy. I not only disliked myself, I hated myself. I tried a few times to destroy myself. When things were said or done that hurt me, the reason it hurt so much was because I knew it was true and I deserved it. I was driving all my friends away - this was distressing too but I didn't know what to do about it.

Although I had a very kind psychiatrist, nothing ever helped me until I came to GROW. I can never repay my kind friend, Dr. G. Johnson, who advised me to come here. Also Fr. Con (one of GROW's Co Founders) and his loyal band of workers and of course the groups. All of these helped me by their kindness and understanding and their friendship. They accepted me as I was. This is my story before I came to GROW.

How GROW helped me.

At my first GROW meeting I was very impressed - people there seemed to care very much for each other. They asked me if I would like to share a problem with them. I told them that they wouldn't understand my problems because I was "different". That didn't impress them at all. Then I said I had too many problems, so I was given a practical task to sort out one problem for the next meeting. I agreed to do that. The following week the members greeted me with a hug. I thought "This won't last long". When they find out what a horrible person I am they won't want to know me. I had little or no personal value and I really believed there was nothing good about me.

Secondly, they remembered my name and not only did they remember that I had a practical task, but it really impressed me that they knew (or remembered) what it was. I thought "these people really care about me and I am going to do whatever they tell me".

It came as a shock to me when I was told by a friend in GROW that how I got sick didn't matter, but it was 'my responsibility to get well'. The fact that I was very mentally ill simply meant that I had to work harder to get well. I would receive help from the members of my GROW group, but I had to be willing to do whatever was necessary to get well. This doesn't mean that I never felt like giving up - I did many times, but the challenge and encouragement I got from the group helped me to 'hang on' from day to day. They told me that 'growth is painful but permanently reward-ing'. There are many parts of the Blue Book that helped me in the early stages. I had to work hard on Personal Value, Mutual Help, The Overall Key to Mental Health, The Four Stabilising Questions, The Three Basic Changes. I could go on telling all the parts that helped me. Gradually my personal value and confidence began to return. I got a lot of support and encouragement from members of the group, but I was also challenged much.

Within a year I was coping well enough to do some part-time voluntary work in the GROW office. In about the same time I had outgrown the need of all medication (after 15 years of constant dependence). I have never, since then, had to return to medication or seek psychiatric help. Of course I still had lots of changing and growing to do, but I was on a winning course and had plenty of time to do it in.

That complete turn around of my life from chronic illness and help-lessness to competence and health took place over twenty years ago. My religious superiors were so impressed by it that they allowed me to take on GROW as my special field of apostolate in the hope that I might pass on to others some of the great benefits I had reaped from it. After 8 years of voluntary work in Sydney, I was incorporated into the staff of GROW International as a fieldworker. I put in 3 years work in Chicago in that capacity - " a finishing school" if ever there was. Then in 1987 I was given the chance to help build GROW in my homeland Ireland, where the movement had begun in 1969. I worked for 2 years in Dublin and then came as a field worker in 1989 to the Midlands carrying GROW's message of hope and health in the very part of Ireland where I was from and grew up.

So much then for the progress of this new life work that has been given me and to which I have become completely dedicated. Taking stock of my life at present I must say that I am much more into education now than I ever was before, but it is very much adult education of the most essential kind, which is the mutual education of shared learning of people for growth to personal maturity or mental health. And since our common journey towards that goal is out of the experience of mental illness, this calls for a lot of compassionate understanding and love, and is consequently very much an extension and deepening of my calling as a Sister of Mercy.

Paddy's Story

My name is Paddy. My family committed me to the local mental hospital in August 1985 and again in August 1986. I believed that there was nothing wrong with me and that they were trying to take the family farm away from me. I had no insight into my illness.

That all changed when I left for London in 1989 where I had a very bad breakdown, thinking the SAS were trying to assassinate me and that I was on the phone to the President of Russia. I returned from London in June 1989 and went into a deep depression and a local doctor recommended GROW to me.

My first few meetings went well, I found the people very helpful and competent. Tom told me how to use distraction techniques which I didn't really understand. At my third meeting I was telling the group that I was going to a nearby holiday resort. A member of the group remarked that my love life was good which caused a laugh. As my pride wouldn't allow anyone to laugh at me I left the group for two years. These were the worst two years of my life- trying suicide and plotting violence against my family. When I returned to GROW in May 1993 I felt that I had nothing left to lose and I really worked at the meetings and the programme.

The parts of the programme that helped me were Step 1 - We admitted we were inadequate or maladjusted to life, Personal Value - 'I can compel my muscles and limbs to act rightly in spite of my feelings', Decentralise and the Prayer of Total Surrender (red book.) The part that helped me the most was What do I Really Want? I got this part early on in GROW and have had to return to it now and again as I had an awful need to impress people. I was given the task to keep contact and to save the turf for the winter fires, not to go to Doolin (a nearby holiday romantic spot) a spot I had driven to every night for six months. The friendships made in GROW and the regular contact give the Growers a great feel for you. You can ring them in a crisis and they understand you. Also they can spot a setback.

After three years in GROW I am now group organiser. I have attended my first O&R meeting and hope that I can put back in some of the help I got. I can now go up to my local village and drink my few coffees and not try and impress anyone by chatting up foreign girls or drinking ten pints with the lads. I have made real friends with the local girls since I stopped trying to chat them up. My mother and my two sisters can rely on me to look after my stock and the farm, and I have a good relationship with them. I'm not interested in going back to Doolin and saving the turf has become a habit.

I am now using the Affirmation of Good and Disturbed Thought and Personal Thought and I am trying to cut out the last of trying to impress people. The group helped me by getting to know me well through the meetings and the very regular contact. They learned how I "tick" and are a step ahead of me.

I need to be consistent at the farming so that my family can rely on me. I need to become more ordinary every day and as group organiser I need to lead by example.

Breda's Story

My name is Breda. I came to GROW nearly eight years ago. I had a lot of family problems at that time which I was unable to cope with. From the beginning I would like to say that I have never been in hospital or on medication for depression. I heard of GROW from a cousin of mine and had given her a commitment to give the programme a "fair go". At this stage I was a complete mess - crying, panic attacks, a doormat for everybody, unable to cope with the smallest tasks. Day to day living had become a nightmare for me. Everyday things, that I had coped with previously without a thought, were now insurmountable problems for me. Because of these symptoms I had completely isolated myself - I didn't want anybody to see the state I was in. I was terrified, I thought I was going "mad".

A few details about my background - I was the youngest of four children. It used to drive me crazy when people said that I must be the "pet", because nothing could have been further from the truth. I always considered myself the "also ran" in the family. I was virtually ignored, fed and dressed of course, but mostly left to my own devices. This situation led to my being very independent and self-sufficient, so hence my terror at my new found inadequacies. My eldest sister was the pet in our house, everything was for her or about her. I hated the very sight of her (jealousy), until I got to know her as an equal in adulthood, and then I grew to love her. I can only remember two occasions in my life when I got a kiss from my mother. Nobody ever told me that I was special or worthwhile. I was very brazen at home and at school, the loudest and cheekiest at work and play. I always had to be the "life and soul" of everything. I know now, with the understanding I have of myself through the GROW programme, that this behaviour was an effort by me to get attention. There is nothing worse than being ignored and even a wallop was better than being invisible. My first impression of GROW was that all the members were either mad, stupid or just weak. But for my commitment to my cousin, I would not have returned. Thank God I did. I wasn't even interested in the friendship offered to me - I didn't want to be friends with "these people". I didn't want to believe that they were stronger than me or that they could actually help me. When the hugging started I nearly freaked out. I must have been one of the most disruptive members that ever joined GROW. At the beginning, I wouldn't open my mouth and I was terrified at the "testing of knowledge" because my concentration was gone completely. I stumbled and stuttered when asked to read something from the Blue Book or the "reading". Next phase, I started to pick "holes" and find fault with the whole philosophy of GROW. I was asked on many occasions to read page 2 of the Blue Book Why am I in GROW?.

After a while, against my will, I began to see the validity of the programme, the basic common sense of it all. I had a huge problem with step 1. - I was willing to admit 'that I was inadequate', basically not coping, but 'maladjusted' - definitely the other members were, but not me. Here was I, a person who had coped alone all my life, who was the solution person for all my family and friends, now having to admit that I had giant flaws in my character and in my way of thinking and acting. I finally made 'the humble admission' and realized that I had a lot of growing to do.

One of the first tasks that I was given was to 'be a person, not an emotional reaction'. Because of my low self-esteem, I was always on the defensive, ready to pounce to defend myself. The Six Rules for Objective Thinking and Control were a great help in combating this problem. I went about all day saying 'I can and I will'. My personal value improved in line with my growth as a person. I began to like myself for the first time in my life. I learned to be able to say "no" and feel good about it. This was a giant step for me. To this day, my favourite part of the programme is The Affirmation of Good, I reckon that it gives us all a clean slate and a fresh start. Also the GROW Aspiration - to become 'gentle builders of a free and whole community'. I want to be a gentle human being, not a loudmouth reactionary. 'Being ordinary' is also very helpful in trying to tackle the daunting task of being a good ordinary human being. I have had a lot of tragedies in my life - both my sisters died at an early age from brain haemorrhages, my best friend died suddenly in the car on our way home from a holiday. These deaths occurred before coming to GROW and I coped okay, looking after everybody else. Now I realize that I never actually dealt with these deaths. My eldest son died in November 1994. On arriving home from a GROW meeting, my husband met me at the door with the words "Barry is dead". I think that I will hear these words forever in my head. My nephew was killed in a car accident in September 1995. The past one and a half years have been very traumatic and painful for me and my family. I experienced despair but with the help of the programme and most of all, my friends in GROW, I have risen again. I dread to think where I would be now without this support, my first reaction being to take to the bed and never rise again. I occasionally find the grief overwhelming but I try to 'resume quickly and without fuss'.' I have learned that the best way to help myself is to help someone else - to 'decentralize'.

I was organizer of my group for two and a half years and am now fieldworker, so it just proves that 'when things go wrong they are meant to go wrong' and that 'a breakdown can be a breakthrough'. As Fr. Stan says in his testimony - a breakdown doesn't happen overnight. There are things in our lives that need to be dealt with and sometimes it takes a breakdown to make us realize this. I have made the most wonderful friends of my life in GROW - "friends for living". I thank each and every one of them. A special word of thanks must go to Helen, who often gave me a "boot" and I didn't even feel it until maybe an hour later, she had such a smile on her face while she was putting the boot in. Also Christine, who helped me to overcome my fear of driving after my son died. And May, my dear, dear friend, who despite her own troubles and the tragic loss of her daughter some months ago, accompanies me on all my field working trips.

I am still working on Acceptance, but getting there, believing that 'the best of life and love and happiness is still ahead'.

Teddy's Story

GROW was something I had heard about a few years before I actually went to a meeting, which I eventually did on a very wet Monday night in October 1993.

The advertisement on the bus seemed to have been written for me: "Anxious, depressed, lonely - we can help". Yes, all those things applied to me, but then I'd hit a good patch, I'd be delighted with life and forget about this thing called GROW again.

I grew up in a rural area called Crookstown, some twenty miles from Cork City, in the middle of the county and had a fairly happy childhood all things considered. Since then I've lived and worked in Cork City and am now earning my crust in Ennis, in the Banner County of Clare. And, believe it or not, GROW in Ireland and myself share the distinction of first seeing the day in 1969. Yes folks, we're both 27 years old!

A lot of things have gone right for me, Thank God, but when some haven't now and again, well they have well and truly gone wrong. I found secondary school to be fairly tough going and, while I did the best I could I suppose, I look back at that time as one that wasn't enjoyable. I was very sensitive to teachers' remarks and this upset me. One teacher often reminded me about my "sad face" and it didn't matter that my results were good in his class. And I wasn't exactly the best of mixers either - you couldn't say I was "one of the lads". But I kept going despite often feeling unhappy in myself. I did the Leaving Cert. in 1988 and went through the same stress, just like everyone else. But less than six weeks after the exams things began to go seriously wrong. I went to Dublin for a first cousin's wedding and, from having looked forward to it during the time leading up to it, I became very uneasy at the reception and wanted to go home as quickly as I could. However, once I did go home, things only got worse. I became full of worry, doubt, anxiety and very unhappy. I couldn't sleep and couldn't even eat, and I thought I was going mad. I went to my local G.P. after a week of "madness" and he gave me tablets. Eventually I had to see a psychiatrist and some weeks later I was admitted as a patient to the G.F. ward (psychiatric unit) in the Cork regional hospital.

I made a good recovery and soon began a course in the R.T.C. in Cork. I was on no medication but I can't say I was one of those college lads who stayed out all night boozing and went to loads and loads of parties. No sir, college is a period that I did not particularly enjoy. How could I because I was still a tense person and, though I could function to a certain level, I was getting very little enjoyment out of life. Going to a pub or disco was out for me and on the odd occasion that I would venture out to these places I'd hate nearly every minute of it. I left college after 3 years in 1991 armed with a diploma in Business Studies and found a job for myself by Christmas.

Again, I drifted on. I must say by now that everything wasn't doom and gloom. I was, and still am, lucky to have some very good friends who were a great deal of help to me. I began to overcome my socialising fears, but things weren't exactly going smoothly at work. While I could get on with the majority of people I found some others a real handful and, unfortunately, one day let my temper get the better of me and struck one of my workmates. This was enough for me to get the sack. Also, at this time, I began going out with a girl and, after six months, she gave me the boot as well! Looking back, it was no surprise as it was far from a perfect relationship. Yet again, I found myself on the ropes and was hospitalised for anxiety/depression in September 1993.

If there was anything good that came out of this period it was perhaps that it made me realise that a spell in hospital or visits to doctors or a dose of tablets were no solution to my particular problems. As well as these medical methods, I tried prayer-groups and meditation and reading some self-help books but I was still struggling. It was now time to "give GROW a go!" Give it a go I did. As I said at the start, I had a certain awareness of GROW. I even rang the Cork office on one occasion but it was after 5 o'clock and I found myself at the end of an answering machine and, even though it was a GROW answering machine, these machines are not quite able to help you with anxiety problems!!! However, I finally came to a GROW meeting on a very wet Monday night in Liberty

St. in October 1993. The first thing I remember was the welcome I got. It was like I had known some of these people for ages and I felt fairly comfortable even from day one. I was so impressed by some people I was convinced they were doctors or social workers - "these people don't have problems" I thought to myself. Yes, my first impressions of GROW were very good. The group advised that there was a group that met on Wednesday night in Wilton which was on my own doorstep at the time. And for the Wilton group I headed the following week.

I stayed with this group for almost twelve months. I can't speak highly enough of the people that represented the core of the group in that time. The help and guidance I got were excellent. GROW is a support group - and support is one thing I definitely got in Wilton. With the co-operation of the group members I began to catch on to the GROW message. The first piece of the programme that I got hold of was explained to me one night over the "cuppa" after the meeting. I was now in GROW for six weeks but I remember going home that night with an extra spring in my step as it had been explained to me that there was a world of difference between how we feel and how we think. So simple, yet I had never grasped it. If I felt lousy, I believed I was lousy, and often acted lousy as a consequence. But now I had a new weapon to beat this army of negative stuff in my head... and I'm still working on it.

Even on a very simple level GROW gave me something to do in these times of unemployment. I looked forward to those 2/3 hours on a Wednesday night and I found a great sense of purpose in being involved in the group setting. Within four months of joining GROW I was able to stop taking medication and haven't taken an antidepressant since. Even before going off medication I found GROW helping me to gain more confidence in myself - sure I was even able to give a blast of "The Wonder of You" at the Christmas social, which was an indication that I was on the right road.

One of the big ways that the Wilton group helped too was that I couldn't help but be affected by the positive things said at the group. Someone would say something in giving a task or piece of the programme to help a person and I'd say to myself "hey, that's good!" It is a thing that's hard to put in words but I think you know what I mean. It is one of the reasons why I still believe so much in GROW and go to meetings. Sometimes all it takes is a few words and 'hey presto' it somehow registers with you. It may happen on a night that the leader hasn't got around to you but you still get benefit from the two hours in the meeting.

The Blue book is a piece of gold. To be honest, I only know a fraction of the book but there are some pieces in this book that should be enlarged and put on billboards around the country to help everyone.

Two pieces that I find of great benefit are:

1. How important is it? (Third Stabilising Question)

If something is troubling you - well, how vital is it?

2. Resume quickly and without fuss..

If something goes wrong, well get on with the next task - don't dwell on errors!

And then there are bits like 'settle for disorder in lesser things, for the sake of order in greater things' and 'deal with behaviour not motives' (4th rule for objective thinking). These are things that one can apply to everyday situations and I'm glad to say that apply them I do. I find they calm me down in what I'd call certain dodgy moments. If I didn't have these little gems I'd still be trying to find a light while cursing the darkness. And it was in GROW that I first came across the Desiderata. That page literally jumped off the book and bit me in the face the night we read it in Wilton. This is something that everyone should look at regularly. And do you know something - it is still biting me in the face! 'With all it's sham, drudgery and broken dreams, it is still a beautiful world'.

Eileen's Story

What led me to GROW:

I joined GROW almost five years ago in October, 1991. At that time I was in a very deep depression. I was attending a psychiatrist in my local clinic. I was prescribed antidepressants by the doctor. The tablets helped restore my sleep pattern and lifted the mood slightly. I knew I needed more than this basic treatment. I was beginning to take charge of my own recovery but I didn't know how to do it on my own. I heard about GROW from a nun with whom I had done a parenting course some years ago. I phoned the GROW office to enquire about the groups and I decided to go along to the Wednesday morning group in Capel Street.

First impressions:

When I went to my first meeting I was confused, I couldn't concentrate, my self esteem was at rock bottom and I felt worthless. These of course were the symptoms of depression but they were very real to me and all I knew at the time.

The first thing that struck me about the group was the friendship. I wasn't sure if GROW could help me as I was so confused and unable to remember or take in fully what was going on. I shared this with the group at the end of the meeting. They gave me a task to come back the following week and to try it for a few weeks before I decided whether it could work or not. I did just that and when I came to my second meeting the affirmation the group gave me for completing my task seemed what I needed to keep coming and I gradually learnt that I was more than my depression.

How the Group helped:

Looking back now I realise that the greatest way in which the group helped was their acceptance of me as I was, unconditionally. They also understood what I was going through which was something my many good friends were unable to do. My new friends understood because they had experienced it themselves. The friendly phone calls and 12th step (meeting people in between meetings) played a big part in my recovery as I could be myself with my new friends. I also found the affirmation I received from the group helped me to build up my self esteem. The group helped by pointing out what I needed to work on when I couldn't see through the fog I was in. The group gave me a sense of belonging and importance. The mutual help aspect of the group also helped to build my self esteem, the fact that I could contribute and help others with their problems. This also helped me to decentralise from my own depression. The GROW groups provided me with leadership skills and gave me the opportunity to practise them both in the group and outside in outreach work.

Practical tasks/Parts of the Programme that helped:

The first piece of the programme I was given to work on was Personal Value - 'No matter how bad my physical, mental or spiritual condition, I am still a human person, loved by God and a connecting link between persons; I am still valuable, my life has a purpose and I have my unique place and my unique part in God's work'. I used to read this piece several times a day. I found it a source of great consolation. This piece and the affirmation I received from the group, having done a task, were the foundation for building my self esteem.

In the beginning I found the simplest of things like getting out of bed, getting the children ready for school etc., very difficult, but using the first of the Three Basic Convictions: 'I can compel my muscles and limbs to act rightly in spite of my feelings' helped me carry out my daily tasks. While I found the friendship in GROW marvellous, I found it difficult at first to be part of the friendly cups of tea because I just felt I wanted to isolate myself. I had to make a special effort to be friendly as the programme says 'keep contact - avoid isolation and keep in friendly touch with other minds' and that 'friendship is the special key to mental health'. As time went on I found it got easier and I began to enjoy the twelfth step and wouldn't miss "the cuppa".

At the start I hated the way I was feeling and couldn't accept it. I found it difficult to accept Step 1: We admitted we were inadequate or maladjusted to life. It seemed to me to be a terrible stigma to be maladjusted, but with the help of a fellow grower, repeatedly telling me it was O.K. to feel like this for now- and it was only for now, not for the rest of my life- this step became acceptable to me. With the acceptance of this step I began to make real progress, to realise that no one is perfect and who isn't maladjusted in some area of life? I also realised that the GROW pro- gramme is a programme for living and can benefit everyone.

On the days when I felt I couldn't do the housework the way I would like to or I couldn't be the mother I wanted to be to my children, in other words perfect, I learnt from the programme that the Overall Key to Men- tal Health is to 'settle for disorder in lesser things for the sake of order in greater things'. The lesser things being, having things perfect and the greater being my mental health.

After about four months in GROW I had made great progress and was asked to lead my first meeting. It was a great boost to my confidence to be able to lead and I certainly found that 'by helping others you help yourself'.

During my recovery I had several set backs. I can remember at one stage feeling so bad, useless and empty. The feelings were so strong I wasn't able to change my thinking. The group gave me the task of changing my talk. I found this very difficult but I really stuck with it. Anytime I wanted to say something negative I would make it more positive or else change the subject to something objective. With the help of the affirmation and reassurance of the group and the passing of time my thinking changed and eventually my feelings improved.

Insights gained:

I first suffered from depression when I was in my early twenties. I didn't know what was wrong with me. I couldn't sleep, had lost interest in eve- rything. I had no confidence and couldn't concentrate on anything. I felt I couldn't do my work and that I was useless. Along with this I be- came very anxious. I didn't know where to turn. Finally a friend referred me to a psychiatrist. This seemed an awful thing at the time to have to do but because my friend knew him I went along. He told me I was suffering from depression and put me on medication. Time went by and I didn't seem to be improving. The anxiety was increasing. I was reaching the end of my "tether". I asked if I could be hospitalised. I didn't know any better at the time, I thought it would be like having a broken leg i.e., hospital would make me better. However, I discovered it wasn't like that.

It was even harder coming out not feeling any better. I was trying to hide the fact that I had been there because of the stigma that went with it. This was 1975. Today I see my hospital stay as merely "time out". I was "labelled" as having endogenous depression but luckily I never accepted this. It didn't make sense to me that I had lived for twenty three years without depression and now they were telling me it was a chemical imbalance. Apart from medication, which helped my anxiety, the most helpful part of my stay in hospital was the friendship of my fellow sufferers. The fact that I found others suffering in the same way reassured me somewhat that I wasn't alone. Today I feel, had I known about GROW when I first got the symptoms of depression, I would never have needed to go to hospital. However, I had to struggle for a good number of years before finding GROW. But I consider myself lucky, I could have missed it. I also see the struggle I had as something I had to go through to gain the insights I have today.

What I needed to change:

When I became well I knew I wanted to stay well. In order to do that I realised that there were certain things about myself I needed to change.

1. I am a perfectionist and I discovered that this had stopped me from doing a lot of things like taking on challenges, as I feared making mistakes. I learned to become ordinary, to drop the ideals and to allow myself make mistakes. Making mistakes in my experience is the real school of learning. It's difficult, but it's also permanently rewarding. The piece 'If a thing is worth doing it's worth doing badly for a start and while you're improving' helped me greatly in this area.

2. I learned to accept myself as I am, just as the group had done initially. 'I am valuable, my life has a purpose and I have my unique place and my unique part in God's work'. I also accept that I have limitations and it is an on-going challenge for me, coping and accepting these. Since I accepted myself as a person with gifts and limitations life has become much easier.

3. I changed my thinking and practised, and still do today Step 8: We learned to think by reason rather than by feelings and imagination. I also had to work hard to 'stop sabotaging'. I had a habit of thinking that when something was going wrong in my life that my life was a disaster. I found the Comforting Paradox helped me here, that 'mostly when things go wrong, they're meant to go wrong - so we can outgrow what we have

to outgrow'.

4. I became aware that some of my relationships were unhealthy, in particular my relationship with my mother. While I was looking after her she was still fulfilling some of my needs. I was still seeking her approval and advice on a lot of decisions in my day to day living. I found it difficult at first not to talk to her about my problems but as time went on I realised that I was better off talking to someone who could see things objectively. I have grown a lot emotionally as a result and today have a very good relationship with my mother.

5. I discovered my depression was mainly due to the fact that I had suppressed my feelings and not dealt with emotional conflicts because I didn't know how. As a child I was smothered with love and not allowed the freedom to express my feelings - in other words be myself. I have done a lot of work on my emotional self and how to handle my feelings. I know now that I must acknowledge them and allow myself to feel them, to go with the flow and then to decentralise, to occupy my mind with something I enjoy. I don't try any more to rationalise them but merely feel them and keep my thinking straight: 'My chief task therefore should be to keep my thinking true and go by what I know, not by how I feel'.

6. I no longer feel the stigma I once felt about being depressed and having to follow the psychiatric path. Why should I stigmatise myself for not knowing the way in or out of this route? That is, until I found GROW and re-educated myself as I have just outlined. I am forever grateful to GROW and my fellow helpers for being there for me.

I became a fieldworker in May 1995. I was a group organiser at the time. By this time I had gladly given a lot back to GROW, as GROW had given much to me. I had reached the stage when I was no longer dependent on the group and I was starting to take stock of where I might go from here when the job of fieldworker came up. I was delighted when I heard I had got the job. I also had some fears as to how I might cope with the work and it's hours etc., as I had a fairly busy life with two children. A year later I can say I find the job challenging and I enjoy the work, especially group visitation and support. There are some frustrations with the job as with any job, but what really keeps me going is the help I see Growers getting from the programme and how it changes them and builds new lives for them. This is what makes my job worthwhile. I didn't have a problem with the transition from organiser to fieldworker. I feel this was due to my years in GROW and the work I had done on building up my personal resources. I still have situations to face that I find challenging. I expect I always will. I found the greatest resources I had to offer as fieldworker were (1) my own story and my experience of coping with depression and (2) my listening presence.

For me the spiritual dimension of my life has been very important in my growth. I feel I could not have grown as I did without it. In order to keep to the right path in this endless journey of growth I meditate. It helps me to let go of my ego and quieten my mind. I find I need time to myself to bring my mind to stillness, to empty everything that has gathered there and then refreshed, to start anew. I feel that life is mostly a blessing and a joy but not without its difficulties. I have found that it is through the difficult periods that we gain most of our growth and these periods have given me great insight and strength. I am firmly convinced that 'when things go wrong they're meant to go wrong so that we can outgrow what we need to outgrow'. Just like a tree we each must find a space to grow and branch out. I am very grateful to have found a space in GROW. I have learnt that 'growth is painful but permanently rewarding' and I look forward to lots more.

Brendan's Story

My name is Brendan, I was born 27 July 1959. To begin my story I will have to go back through the days of my childhood and when I look back I can remember some very happy times which nothing can take away. Like many of my fellow Growers I was very sensitive which in time led me to being insecure and lacking in self confidence. This made my thinking go right "off beam".

At school I had periods of being bullied and I especially remember the verbal abuse which was much worse than the physical abuse. My mother suffered from poor health throughout my childhood and into my teens. She died when I was 16 years of age. I left primary school at 14 and with no real pressure from my parents, I did not further my education. I went out working in a factory and this is where some of my first real problems started. We were all young people which meant there was a lot of messing and joking. One day, for a joke, I passed around a cup of coffee in a coke bottle which was left near a machine that made metal stoppers. I then started to THINK that I had harmed the people who had a taste, even when reason should have told me the mixture would be harmless. After that my thinking became very fearful and obsessive. I suffered from phobias such as fear of germs and chemicals which came from a deep insecurity, into which I have now gained a great insight from the GROW programme.

I married Marion when I was 21 years of age and had some good years, keeping myself active in sport such as running and karate. We had our first child, Elaine in 1982, Johnathan in 1984 and Shane in 1991. It was in the following years that the depression really started to get worse with long periods of feeling "down and out". It was Christmas 1992 that my life came tumbling down on me. I felt so burnt out and at a dead end. I went back to my G.P., totally desperate and stressed out. He was a great help and very understanding. He put me on medication and gave me sleeping pills. These helped me cope but could not help me change my thinking. I also asked my G.P. if he knew of any support group that could help me with my problems. He suggested AWARE. The meetings were held in Galway which was a long distance away. A few weeks passed and one Sunday, looking through the Clare Champion I saw the notice for GROW meetings on Monday night in Ennis. Just seeing that there was a support group gave me a glimmer of hope. I told Marion and she said to give it a go. I remember the first night I went to GROW, I did not know what to expect. My first impression was the great support and friendship the members offered to each other. I must admit that I could not understand the GROW programme. The group told me to give it at least three months. Going away I had mixed feelings. Marion gave me great support and encouraged me to return. To this day I thank God I did. After only three meetings I started to talk and this helped me a lot - they could understand what I was going through. After a while, when I had started to get better I got involved and tried my best to help other people. This helped me to take the spotlight off myself and also taught me that I was not the only one with problems. It was a fantastic boost to listen to the seasoned Growers who had come through serious illness and were now coping well and getting on with their lives.

The practical tasks that I was given were mainly to do with dealing with the phobias - to let Marion lock the doors at night because I had the habit of checking and rechecking. Also I was encouraged to keep in contact with the other Growers. Step 8 helped me the most - We learned to think by reason rather than by feelings and imagination. Also The Three Basic Convictions, 3 Practical Points for Control and Decentralise.

The insights I have gained come from the Steps and the Programme which has taught me to put back one thing into my thinking that was missing, which was REASON. 12th step work meant you could talk to someone when maybe you were struggling and get advice and a part of the programme to help you. Also you could just phone another Grower for a chat or to help them along.

This brings me to where I am now. I'm coping a lot better, off medication, my relationship with Marion has improved greatly. I am much more relaxed now and not nearly so anxious, just taking it one day at the time.

I have more work to do but it is like a jigsaw coming together, bit by bit. What I am using now is The Overall Key to Mental health. I'm using this to help me at work. Also 7 More Keys for Understanding Feelings - 'there is no natural way to good feelings'. I'm using these to put order in my day and to 'beat the bluff'.

Frances's Story

My name is Frances. I have been a GROW member for the past 2 years. When I look back at my state of mind 2 years ago, it's hard to believe that I am still the same person. I was very unhappy and on the verge of a nervous breakdown. The previous year had been a very hard year for me emotionally. I had, after a lot of tests, been told that I couldn't have children. I was devastated to say the least, as I love children, and had hoped to have at least three. Our next option was to adopt. I had no problem making up my mind to do this as it didn't matter to me or my husband whether the child was ours naturally or not. We just wanted a chance to be parents. I felt my life would never be complete if I couldn't be a mother. However this too was wrong for us as we were told we were over the age limit for adoption. I was only 34 and my husband 38, but due to the small amount of children available for adoption, the age limit was brought down. We were only a couple of months over the qualifying age but nothing could be done to change the rules. I couldn't accept the fact that I would never have a child - all I could do was cry. I felt a failure as a woman. My health started to deteriorate, I couldn't eat or sleep. Work became a nightmare. This went on for months. I used to pray at night for God to take me. I hated the world. I got so run down that the doctor sent me for blood tests for suspected diabetes. When the tests came back clear I was actually disappointed- at least that would have been an answer to my health problems. On my doctor's advice I took time off work- he told me I was suffering from depression. My job began to get me down- I was unable for the pressure. Eventually I resigned, after being there for nearly 7 years. This only added to my feelings of inadequacy.

I was also carrying a lot of baggage from the past. My father was an alcoholic and a gambler. Anyone who comes from a background like that will know the effect it has on your life. We lived in poverty. My father could be very argumentative when he was drunk and when he was sober he didn't want us around. He showed us no love at all but thank God we got plenty from my mother. I carried a lot of resentment for my father and blamed him for everything that went wrong with my life. I had no confidence and I was very insecure, unable to cope with life's problems.

When I found GROW my first impression was of how friendly and open the members were. Being so shy, I found it hard to sit in a room full of people. I thought I would never have the courage to open my mouth. But I felt understood and I knew that I was going to find help there. The first part of the programme I was given was Acceptance. I had to accept my situation and work on the positive things in my life. I also had a lot of work to do on my personal value. I read page 7 of the Blue Book every morning, as I was told to do. These two parts of the programme changed my feelings towards myself and my situation. I could see a future ahead of me. However, I still tended to live in the past, especially where my feelings for my father were concerned. One night, during the Middle Routine, we had the reading on Resentment. It explained that resentment is like poison, it can actually make you sick. It also explained that if you have resentment for someone you can do yourself real harm. We can't live in the past, if we do we can't enjoy today. The reading suggested that we look at the life of the person we resent and try to see what caused them to act the way they did. I now feel sorry for my father- he missed out on so much in his life. He died aged 46 without ever having a real relationship with any of his family. Now I pray for him. I found the Affirmation of Good very helpful - 'We freely forgive from our hearts those who have wronged or failed us, including our own selves'.

I am now waiting for a call to go to Russia to adopt a little boy. I would never have had the courage to go through all the waiting and hoping without my friends in GROW. I will never forget the support and encouragement I got from the group. The friendship in GROW is wonderful, just to know you can pick up the phone when you need someone to talk to, makes the ups and downs of life bearable. The part of the programme I am working on at the moment is Let go and let God, which is helping me to cope with my sister's death. She died a short time ago, leaving 5 children. I believe that God is helping us all right now. I also believe that

God led me and my mother to GROW two years ago. As I said earlier, I used to ask God to take me out of this world. Now I am looking forward to the rest of my life because I know I can enjoy the good and cope with the bad. I want to say thank you for enabling me to take control of my life.

Nuala's Story

My name is Nuala. I joined GROW in 1979. I was very sick, diagnosed with clinical depression, chronic anxiety and being neurotic. I was attending my psychiatrist for nine years and on quite a lot of medication.

I was living in fear of everything and everyone. Those nine years I did not leave my house except for the visits to the psychiatrist. I slept most of the time and in my waking moments I would sit in a chair with racing thoughts and responding to no one.

I was introduced to GROW by a friend. I had never heard of GROW and was reluctant to go. The advice from my friend was to give it at least three months and then make a decision to stay or leave. I suppose I was fed up with everyone giving me advice, but I went along with my friend to my first GROW meeting in Inchicore. I must confess it didn't make much impression on me as I was so full of medication, but I noticed a buzz with everyone there reporting on practical tasks they had received from the previous meeting and a little reading to go with it. The friendship was wonderful and at the end of the meeting the organiser was arranging for all of us to meet up for coffee during the week which is called in GROW 12 Step work. It's really to get to know the whole person, not just the problem person.

When I told them my story, all of them could identify with me and I was started on my journey to personal growth and maturity. GROW is a 12 step programme and I started to learn and adopt GROW's 12 steps of growth.

Within a few months I started to improve with the help of the group as I was reminded constantly 'you alone can do it, but you can't do it alone'. I had to work on the Three Basic Changes: change of thinking, change of talk and change of relationships. My thinking got positive. I started to 'emphasize what is rather than what isn't', counting my blessings, thinking good about myself and others. I learned 'my life had a purpose and I was valuable', I could 'do what ordinary good people could do'. I regained my sense of humour and my relationships became equal. The biggest problem I had to face was taking responsibility for my own life, so within two years, with my psychiatrist's approval, I was off all medication and bade farewell to my doctor.

I had recovered from my breakdown but the biggest task was ahead and that was to grow to maturity. I found this pretty awesome as GROW defines maturity as 'coming to terms with oneself, with others and with life as a whole'. 'We describe a mature person as having a true mind, a loving heart and a strong character. The five foundations of maturity are understanding, acceptance, confidence, control and love'.

Mutual help is a lifelong process. So I became very involved in GROW on a voluntary level, still getting help at my own group. In July 1994 a vacancy arose for a part-time fieldworker. I applied and was successful in being given the job. I found the challenge of working for GROW a little difficult. This was a new area for me and I sometimes wondered if I had made the right decision. But one year on with the help of the other GROW staff I know my decision was right.

The difficulty for me as a fieldworker was learning to control my time keeping, most times I was out of breath going nowhere. Again with the help of my group and staff and friends I was advised to make a plan for the week and stay with it as far as possible. My reading to help me with this was 'Peace is the Tranquillity of Order'. This helped me a great deal and I became less anxious and I realised I was the same Nuala with the same strengths and weaknesses as before.

As I write this testimony I realise the rewards of being a fieldworker outweigh the difficulties. I help arrange training in our own Region, arrange GROW community weekends and get to know each Grower on a more personal and equal level. My thanks to all GROW staff for their help and support in my weaker moments and I know 'the best in life, love and happiness is ahead of me.'

AFTERWORD

The title of this collection of testimonies alerts the reader to the spiritual nature of the work of GROW. I chose the word testimony carefully as, in my opinion, the moving accounts of each person's unique journey are placed tenderly in the context of all the other accounts. In this way each testimony bears witness to the accounts of the others. What emerges is a sense of the remarkable human communion that is GROW.

One does not immediately connect the domain of spirituality with the pragmatic aims of this network of people. However, as each story unfolds a glow of spirituality emerges through the words themselves and through the narratives of courage, tenacity, pain, support and joy. Enveloped by this sense of human strength and resourcefulness I, as a privileged commentator, began to wonder what it was that might give rise to such an aura of spirituality.

What I identified with through my reading of this remarkable collection is the importance of a community of support and simple, immediately usable goals and principles. Most of the accounts speak to the life support they find in GROW as crucial in their journey from isolation to social connection. It is as if through the extension of secular connections that sacred links are forged. Through these connections and links the principles, contained in the three books of GROW, continue to be generated and regenerated by the whole community. The forging of principles in this way seems to create a potent context in which authentic expressions of self find voice and are nurtured. As I was reading I also had the sense that the principles are mottoes for living and indeed many use them as mantras along the route. One principle I will particularly remember is 'You alone can do it but you can't do it alone'. It will serve me well, when I begin to imagine that I can do everything by myself or that my clients can do likewise. We all need a community of support to hold us in our dark and joyful moments - a space where we can find our voices and be heard for who we are.

What I offer here are the themes which stood out for me. These may be different from those which will be significant for the members of GROW themselves or indeed for other readers. As such I offer them tentatively and with respect for those who know much better than I do what is important in their lives. I thank the writers and hope that from now on I can be a more respectful witness to the truths of those who seek my help.

Imelda McCarthy

Dr. Imelda McCarthy PhD.
Lecturer in Social Work UCD and Psychotherapist.

EPILOGUE

This is an important book that deserves to be widely read. This is not the case because GROW is very often effective in helping people recover from debilitating mental illnesses (it often can be). It is not the case because health care professionals need reminding that they deal with situated human beings rather than abstract problems susceptible to quick technical fixes (some of them do indeed require this reminder). Finally, it is not the case because the stories themselves are intrinsically interesting from the perspective of medical anthropology (in fact, they are). This is an important book because it shows all of us involved in either delivering services to distressed individuals or collaborating with them to advance human knowledge about their experiences how often limited and limiting are our senses of their lives and problems.

Unfortunately, even if read, it will still be too easy for the volumes in this series not to be accorded the respect that they deserve. They stand in danger of being read as merely the soft window-dressing around the harder issues of chemically imbalanced brains and the development of even more powerful pharmaceutical interventions.

Instead, this and the other volumes in the Soul Survivor Series should be required reading for psychiatrists, GPs, nurses, social workers, and health services researchers because they place the experience of distress and the experience of seeking relief for distress firmly within the frame of self-authored life histories.

We are developing evidence from surprisingly varied cultural contexts that a critical aspect of successfully living with chronic conditions, as well as acute illnesses of uncertain duration, is the ability to develop a story that comes to a satisfactory resolution. Further, we are also coming to understand that the inability to develop a satisfactory life story is implicated in poor outcomes for many disorders. One of the most robust findings in cross-cultural psychiatry, for example, is the relatively poorer prognosis for people in developed societies diagnosed as suffering from one of the group of schizophrenias in comparison with those so diagnosed in less developed countries. It has been suggested in recent years that these poorer outcomes in the developed world (at least in the United States) can be at least partially explained by the narrative overlap between disease and identity.

Essentially, one becomes, for example, "a schizophrenic" often with very limited means of moving away from this unhappy congruence of self and disorder.

These stories are articulate and moving accounts of this struggle between identity and illness. They show how the experience of distress, seeking help to alleviate it, and struggling to get beyond it occurs in worlds that are meaningfully constituted through narratives. This sense of people in distress being interesting to listen to is one of the most pressing issues in the delivery of health services. The irony is that while so much of the challenge in health care is social — to enhance the capacity of individuals to perform desired roles and activities — the main thrust of the health enterprise is substantially reductionist, treating complex socio-medical problems as if they were amenable to simple technical fixes. Nonetheless, study after study demonstrates that people's perceptions are powerful indicators of their future health, even their mortality, but such subjective features are too often viewed by physicians as soft and unimportant.

The Soul Survivor Series developed by GROW should help to change such perceptions. These volumes will assist all concerned with individuals who have been diagnosed with mental illnesses to appreciate how the experiences of distress and relief from distress is woven into the warp and woof of social life. Further, they show that one of the best ways of understanding these densely-woven threads is through first-person accounts of these experiences.

A. Jamie Saris

A. Jamie Saris, PhD
Department of Anthropology,
National University of Ireland,
Maynooth.